YOUR DAILY WALK
WITH THE GREAT MINDS

PRAISE FOR
YOUR DAILY WALK WITH THE GREAT MINDS

Your Daily Walk With The Great Minds... is a highly intimate and engaging philosophy...very strongly recommended...for its invaluable grasp of worldly study and in-depth analysis of the surrounding experience.

MidWest Book Review

"The author did not create an inspirational tool, but a sagacious wormhole for extraordinary change by combining valuable elements sparking synergy. A must-have book, destined best seller, and powerful vehicle ready to fly."

Recommended and Reviewed in the
Mindquest Review, by Lightword Publishing.

"More than simply daily meditations, Your Daily Walk provides priceless pearls of wisdom, meditations, and opportunities for personal journaling. This gem of a book is a wonderful traveling companion throughout the year, offering opportunities for spiritual growth and enrichment. I highly recommend it."

David J. Powell, Ph.D.,
President International Center for Health Concerns, Inc. and Institute of Mental Health, Beijing Medical University, Beijing China. Also, Author of *Playing Life's Second Half.* www.ich-us.org.

"Mr. Singer's masterpiece offers a path to shape your day and dares you to risk and grow—to meet your true potential. If you thirst for true meaning in life, *Your Daily Walk with the Great Minds* by Richard A. Singer, Jr. is a necessity. Highly Recommended."

Sue Vogan, BookPleasures.com

"This is a powerful book, a tool for inner peace. For those who are looking to make a change, or just a journal to enjoy, for those who are into learning from the teachers in their lives along their chosen path and for those who have never given spiritual growth a single thought, this book is for you. Enjoy it, give it as a gift, and watch the transformation of humanity."

Heather Froeschl, BookReview.com

"Our true self is often suppressed due to the many distractions life thrusts upon us. Mr. Singer has embarked on a mission that can awaken us, daily, in the pursuit of liberating who we are and what we can become. This book will inspire you to accomplish beyond the limits you have currently set for yourself and help you see who you really are."

Scott L. Taylor,
Author—*The Opportunity in Every Problem*

"This outstanding book guides the reader toward the sunlight of the spirit. This book is a must read. Thank you Richard your book has truly touched my spirit, and I know it will reach the hearts of many people."

Dr. Katie Evans,
Therapist and Author of
Addiction and Trauma Related Books

"I think it's an excellent gift to yourself or to anyone on your list who is intentional about personal growth and spiritual development. I can only hope that Mr. Singer creates more versions of this wonderful concept so that a reader can fill several volumes over the years."

Ron McCray,
Author of *The Tao of God*

"Many of us are familiar with the great thoughts and thinkers in the personal development field, but we need to be inspired every day if they are to have any lasting effect on our lives. *Your Daily Walk* provides exactly this inspirational service in an easy to use and practical format that will help people to stay focused on what they want from life."

Tom Butler-Bowdon,
Author of "*50 Self-Help Classics*" &
"*50 Spiritual Classics*"

There is an enormous, generous energy in the universe — available to anyone who opens their hearts, minds and souls. In *Your Daily Walk with the Great Minds*, Richard Singer is both our guide and fellow traveler on a journey toward growth and fulfilment. He weaves his skill and insight into daily meditations and thought provoking questions that are inspired by quotes from great men and women to create a process for transformation that does not feel onerous or difficult. This is not a book meant to be read and put on the shelf. It is a book to be kept handy—beside you on your nightstand, in your desk drawer. It is a book of life lived to its fullest potential, and of human spirit at its most resilient. It is a book that will become a part of your life.

Theresa Peluso,
Co-author,
Chicken Soup for the Recovering Soul

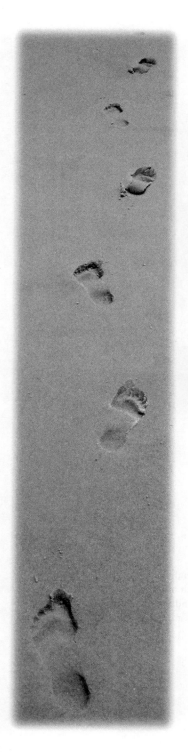

Your Daily
Walk with
the
Great Minds

Richard A. Singer, Jr.

inkstone

Cover: DARKHORSE DESIGN
e-mail: darkhorse@chariot.net.au
Cover Image: © Jimmy Lopes

Your Daily Walk with the Great Minds
Copyright © 2007 Richard A. Singer, Jr.
Inkstone Press Pty Ltd, Australia

ISBN: 978 0 9803180 4 3

Printed in Malaysia

ACKNOWLEDGMENTS

In the words of the brilliant writer Paulo Coelho, "When somebody wants something the whole Universe conspires in their favor." This is an accurate description of the process of this book. First and foremost I must express my gratitude for the eternal and all-loving Universal Source that has allowed me to bring this book into the world in order to help the transformation of humanity. Secondly, I must thank my entire family, without them I would not be the person I am today. They also labored endlessly to promote the first edition and genuinely believed in me. I also have incredible gratitude for the initial book reviewers and authors who gave my work a chance and had faith in me as a writer. They are: Heather Froeschl, from BookReview.com and Quilldipper.com, Sue Vogan, from BookPleasures.com, Larry Hehn, Author of *Get the Prize: Nine Keys for a Life of Victory*, David Powell, Author of *Playing Lifes Second Half*, Tom Butler-Bowden, Author of *50 Self help Classics*, Ron McRay, Author of *Tao of God*, and Theresa Peluso, Co-Author of *Chicken Soup for the Recovering Soul*. I also need to express my gratitude for those authors and reviewers who did not have time to review my work. You are more important than anyone else because you challenged me to persist with passion and determination. Thank you for your help in my personal growth process. Finally, I must thank Loving Healing press for becoming involved in the growth and success of this book. It will have a lasting effect on countless lives.

This book is dedicated to all of humanity.
Each human being that walks this earth is just
as valuable and precious as the next.

FOREWORD

The secret of a good book is that it reaches into the reader's heart and touches him at a deeper level. You, the reader, know when the words on the page are true, for they have always been true for you. "I knew that. I guess I've always known that," is the response we give when we connect words with the heart. Anne Lamott says, "Good writing is about telling the truth." Good books help us pay attention to and communicate about what is truly going on for us in life, what is Truth.

Good books also communicate the wisdom of the sages through the ages. Some age-old wisdom sustains us through the hours, days or years of sunshine that lights up our lives. Some wisdom is aimed at the cold dark places within, the water under the frozen lakes of our lives. These are the times when we need light and encouragement. The Buddha said life is 10,000 joys and 10,000 sorrows. Either way, the wisdom of the ages shines on the secluded, camouflaged holes of our lives, helping us to step and live through the brambles of our life.

Life is like a giant recycling machine. The wisdom learned from other people's life dramas gets recycled back across time. The good wisdom of the ages is already out there, waiting to be told and received in fresh, new and wild ways. Mark Twain said that Adam is the only person that could be 100% certain that nobody before him had done or said what he did or said. Ever since the Garden of Eden, we have been recycling the wisdom of the ages, which gives us new light and life as if we are hearing it again for the first time.

Wendell Berry, the curmudgeon Kentuckian poet, describes this process wherein we, after all these years, find something that makes sense to us, again, but as if we'd never heard it before:

> *Sometimes hidden from me*
> *In daily custom and in trust,*
> *So that I live by you unaware*
> *As by the beating of my heart,*
> *Suddenly you flare in my sight,*
> *A wild rose blooming at the edge*
> *Of thicket, grace and light*
> *Where yesterday was only shade,*
> *And once again I am blessed, choosing*
> *Again what I chose before.*

How does that happen? Truth and wisdom have a way of harvesting and integrating the joys, sorrows, glories, mediocrity, and even evil of a lifetime, transfiguring everything. Wisdom goes before and behind us, breaking through and consuming into life the dyings of a lifetime.

Wisdom of the past lights up the spiral path of life which, for most of us, is largely unmarked and not easy to follow. Wisdom gives us the light to allow us to transform our pain. If we do not transform our pain, we transmit it. So, what transforms pain? I have come to see that transformed people transform people. They offer us a vision of a new set of values, a deeper understanding of ourselves, a greater appreciation of our own innate and acquired wisdom, and most importantly, a deeper capacity to love.

So what transforms people then? Sometimes change happens when something appeals to our intellect. Sometimes we change when we learn a new skill or an idea. We always change when we are confronted with love that is conveyed to us in the silence and sounds of others. Love always transforms people.

So, good books and sound wisdom (prior and present) convey to us a deep abiding presence, a sense of a hidden wholeness. Thomas Merton spoke of this as returning to our true self. Buddhists call this our original nature. Quakers named it our Inner Teacher. Jews through the ages have spoken of this as the spark of the Divine. Psychologists speak of our identity and integrity. I will call it our soul that yearns to be rooted in something Else that tells us the truth about ourselves and our world. It gives us life. T.S. Elliot said:

> We shall not cease from exploration
> and the end of all our exploring
> will be to arrive where we started
> and know the place for the first time.

True wisdom does not seek to fix anything. In it there is no saving, no advising, and no setting the person straight. True wisdom simply holds us faithfully in a space where we can listen to our inner teacher and find truth. It offers us an eternal conversation about things that matter, conducted within and around us, with passion and an air of discovery.

In this process of transformation, a response is required of us. What are our thoughts, meditations, and emotions as we hear the words of wisdom of the past? At some point we are asked "How do you feel about that?" Writing down our responses through journaling, we engage in a spiritual discipline. Journaling is not the same thing as a simple diary of activities, a systematic listing of events. Journaling asks us to record our reactions to the words of wisdom, chronicling the spiritual odyssey we are taking, day-by-day and hour- by-hour. Journaling provides us a means of meditation wherein we become engaged in the conversations with the authors of the wisdom.

There is something in the physical act of writing that releases our creative responses and leads to self-understanding. Regularity in journaling is essential as a way of providing us structure, form and consistency to our meditations. The time for journaling is less important than the regularity of it. Ideally, it can become a daily practice. The first step of journaling is to relax into the space, to prepare ourselves for the spirit that is at work within us, drawn out by the wisdom we've read. We need to breathe deeply, finding ways of our own choosing to clear our mind of other things so that the words can wash over us, like the cascading waters of a morning shower.

A disciplined form of growth comes as daily readings. *Your Daily Walk with the Great Minds* by Richard A. Singer, Jr. offers a daily guide and disciplined way to allow the wisdom of the past and present to wash over us, allowing the reader to enter his inner spiritual world and to reflect on how he responds to this wisdom. This book can transform your life, especially if you accept the daily discipline of reading, relaxing, and reflecting on the words.

*Your Daily Walk...*is packed with the wisdom of great minds, from Dale Carnegie to Anton Chekhov, from great thinkers like Euripides to Ralph Waldo Emerson to Einstein to Thomas Edison. It gives us the thoughts of Henry David Thoreau to Harriet Beecher Stowe. We follow the ideas of great poets from Walt Whitman to Robert Frost. This gem of a book moves us through the diversity of words from people such as Henry Ford, Sigmund Freud, Vince Lombardi, Mahatmas Gandhi, Aristotle, Augustine, Martin Luther King, Jr., Abraham Lincoln, St. Augustine, Mother Teresa and John Paul Sartre. It encompasses the wisdom of writers as diverse as Hindu and Buddhist texts, the Jewish Talmud, and philosophers ranging from Lao-Tzu and Confucius to Milton Berle.

The wisdom encapsulated in this book can transform your life, especially if you soak in the words and practice the daily discipline of journaling and Meditation, as the book allows. This is a gem filled with daily opportunities to grow for its words are true. They will resonate with your head, heart, and soul.

David J. Powell, Ph.D.

INTRODUCTION

"Words are the physicians for the mind diseased."

— Aeschylus

I have been chosen by a much higher source than myself to unveil the components of my successful life transformation with those who are receptive to it across the globe. The specific books, Quotations, Meditations, Affirmations, and Ask Yourself segments expressed throughout this book had the power to raise me up from the streets and transform me from a homeless drug addict in desperate pain to a successful human being living the life of my dreams on a tropical island in the Caribbean.

I am providing you with my foundation for healing which was inspired by the energy of this vast and miraculous universe. Each Quote, Meditation, Ask Yourself, and Affirmation is meant to be applied each specific day of your life and in each exact situation that you encounter. Absolutely nothing happens in this world by coincidence and the same goes for this daily guide for personal growth and transformation. These daily guides will synchronize your soul with your desired journey of success and align you with your universal purpose. If you allow yourself to remain mindful of each moment you will certainly witness the synchronicity and perfection of the sacred puzzle of your life. Everything in your life fits together in harmony with the Divine Source of being.

"Most collectors collect tangibles. As a quotation collector, I collect wisdom, life, invisible beauty, souls alive in ink."

— Terri Guillments

This book is not meant to be read like a traditional self-help book. A majority of the self-help books that we read are quickly discarded by our minds and never genuinely applied to our life's journey. This book is a daily guide for personal growth and genuine, spiritually grounded success for you and the world around you. Each day you will enter the inner world of one of the universe's most influential minds and be gently guided to living a life your higher-self desires for you and a life of immense contentment and peace. This book contains basic principles that will transform your life and assist in your journey of success and prosperity. An added benefit is the profound effect it will have on those human beings around you and the world as a whole. The changes you make will benefit the entire Universe. Thus, the world will be changed by each person practicing the principles of this book one day at a time. My hope is that enough people will choose to apply these principles diligently and persistently in order to bring about a tremendous and astonishing change in the world around us. With much effort, humanity will begin to change one day at a time. Remember, keep your thoughts in the day and be mindful of every moment that you experience. This approach is centered on the now, which is all we have. The daily Quote, Meditation, personal Ask Yourself, and the Affirmation will guide you on your journey each day and will align your life with the blueprint imbedded in your soul. Trust in this, believe in this, and conscientiously practice this daily program and you will be amazed at what you will achieve in your life and who you will become. I wish you the best on the most influential journey of your life. Pass this book on when finished, recommend it, and give it as a gift. I cannot wait to see the transformation that this book has on your life and humanity as a whole.

"Each night I go to sleep I die and the next morning when I wake up I am reborn again."

— M. K. Gandhi

This daily guide combines strategies and personal growth techniques to most effectively help you transform your life. These strategies and techniques have been shown in recent research to enhance the change process when individuals have the internal desire to do so. I will briefly describe these specific aspects of the guide. My hope is that you can utilize them in order to maximize the change in your life and increase your ability to transform humanity.

1. Modeling—The quotations from these great minds will give you the opportunity to do what they did to achieve maximum success and greatness. You have the ability and capacity to believe what they believed , think how they thought, and to live how they lived. You have the incredible opportunity to be escorted by these great minds and carry on their success and brilliance in your own life. The quotes contained in this guide are the keys they left us to unlock the hidden radiance in our lives and the universe. I think it's common sense to do what other human beings have done if you want what they achieved. William James, the famous psychologist, recommended this years ago when he said, "act as if." Pretend that you are successful; imagine that you are who and what you want to be and simulate that in your daily life. No one will know you are pretending; if they do, who cares anyway. Act like this each day and you will become it.

2. Bibliotherapy—This is very simple, reading helps people gain knowledge, insight, and understanding to change. Reading the monthly suggested books gives you the additional tools you need to succeed and become the person you yearn to be. Be sure to read mindfully, take notes, and apply the principles within the books to your life.

3. Mindfulness—This aspect teaches you and affords you the opportunity to experience the gift of the moment and the preciousness of life. This asks you to be open and truly live each moment of the day while applying the daily guidance provided in this book. Apply it and practice it throughout the day and this will make each quote, each Meditation, and each principle a permanent element of your being.

4. Journaling—This book contains a specific section (Ask Yourself)each day for you to express your thoughts, your plan on application of the Meditation, your feelings, and your current beliefs. This section is provided for you to express whatever comes to mind. Journaling is an important part of the program and has proven to be very effective in change and the healing of human beings.

5. Visualization—Each day, I encourage you to visualize yourself living and practicing each Meditation and quotation. Visualize your growth spiritually, mentally, and emotionally. Visualize your transformation, your future success, and the life you long for. If you truly visualize and imagine these results, you are certain to achieve them.

6. Affirmations—An affirmation is provided for each day. Read this, internalize it, believe it, and apply it throughout your daily journey. Write it down, put it in your pocket and repeat it to yourself as your day unfolds and consistently remind yourself of it. This aspect of the guide is important in changing your beliefs and actions as well as providing further guidance along your daily passage.

I hope you find this program helpful to you. It changed my life and I continue to practice these techniques on a daily basis, making my life and being only that much better. Welcome to your daily journey and the beginning of the evolution of your eternal being.

Suggested Books of the Month

January:
Power of Positive Thinking —Norman Vincent Peale

February:
Power of Intention —Dr. Wayne Dyer

March:
As a Man Thinketh —James Allen

April:
Infinite Self —Stuart Wilde

May:
The Road Less Traveled —M. Scott Peck

June:
The Alchemist —Paulo Coelho

July:
Don't Sweat the Small Stuff —Dr. Richard Carlson

August:
Tuesdays with Morrie —Mitch Albom

September:
Seven Spiritual Laws of Success —Deepak Chopra

October:
Man's Search for Meaning —Victor Frankl

November:
Greatest Salesman in the World —Og Mandino

December:
The Five People you Meet in Heaven —Mitch Albom

JANUARY 1 *"It's not that some people have will power and some don't. It's that some people are ready to change and others are not."*

— James Gordon, M.D.

Meditation: It's a new year and that offers the possibility of a refreshing commencement and the creation of a revitalized life. Today make a commitment to live in the moment and be the artist of your exceptional, more purposeful, and passionate life. Always remember that you are the artist and you have the freedom to paint the masterpiece of your existence any way you wish. There are infinite possibilities in your life. Within you lies the power to create the life you desire.

Ask Yourself: What is your initial plan and desire for the invention of your new life?

I Affirm: Today, I will sincerely believe in my ability to transform my life and I will begin taking action this very moment.

⊷⊶⊸◯◯⊶⊷

JANUARY 2 *"He who is afraid of doing too much always does too little."*

— German Proverb

Meditation: Often, life becomes overwhelming and we simply need a reprieve to relax and gather our thoughts. Allow yourself to relax and replenish your energy to move forward. Be certain not to allow yourself to get stagnate and forget about the dreams and aspirations you are working towards. The answers that we seek often come in times of silence, when we unite with the energy of the universal consciousness. Think of this time as productive relaxation, which will act as a catalyst for further growth and success.

Ask Yourself: What will you do to quiet your mind and regain your strength today? (Try something new like a swim in the lake, a walk in the woods, a hot bath, or create an activity that is sure to relax your mind and soul.)

I Affirm: Today, I will become one with the silence of the Universe and engage in the revitalization of my heart, mind, and soul.

JANUARY **3**   *"Never neglect the little things in life."*

— Og Mandino

Meditation: It's extremely common to neglect saying, "I love you," to your family, to forget about an important anniversary, neglect the true essence of a flower or the sunset, or just forget that love and kindness are the basic and most vital ingredients in your life. Step out of the rapid pace of society and remember what is genuinely important to you. (I'll bet true importance does not lie in the kind of car you drive or how much your phone bill was last month.) Bring into consciousness, remain mindful of the truly important things in your life, and make an effort to show appreciation for these priceless things today.

Ask Yourself: What are you going to do today that you often neglect in your daily life? (Tell a family member that you love them, write a letter to a friend, be kind to yourself and others, enjoy a beautiful sunset, etc.) These simple things will make a huge difference in the quality and satisfaction of your life.

I Affirm: Today, I will escape the chaos of the world and make the time to cherish what is sincerely important to my inner most being.

JANUARY **4**   *"No race can prosper till it learns that there is as much dignity in tilling a field as in writing a poem."*

— Booker T. Washington

Meditation: Every human being has their special place in this world. We, as members of the human race, must acknowledge this fact and express gratitude for the diverse population of human beings and their unique skills. Everybody, from the human being that washes dishes to the individual that runs a Fortune 500 company, has their distinct place and purpose in this Universe. We are all members of the same race and have a responsibility to treat each other the way we expect to be treated. If this world is to evolve, we need to honor the connection between all of humanity and come together as one with a single purpose; the purpose of peace and unity.

Ask Yourself: What is your place in the Universe and how do you plan to fulfill your ultimate purpose of helping other human beings? Do you recognize the equality of all human beings?

I Affirm: Today, I will contemplate how I can help other human beings in my daily life and begin this significant work immediately.

JANUARY 5   *"Diligence is the mother of good luck."*

— **Benjamin Franklin**

Meditation: Good Luck is often prayed for, searched for, and consistently desired throughout our lives. The concept of "luck" is external to us and beyond our immediate control, however, through conscientiousness and perseverance we can create our own form of "good luck" based on our inner selves, which is in our control. You may continue to depend on that "luck" finding you or, perhaps, make a decision to practice determination in everything you do and manifest your self-created destiny. The choice is up to you.

Ask Yourself: How will you practice your "luck finding" skills today, rather than waiting for it to come to you?

I Affirm: Today, I will rely on my higher-self to create positive changes in my life, rather than sitting around waiting for "Good Luck".

JANUARY 6   *"Its not that I'm so smart, it's just that I stay with problems longer."*

— **Albert Einstein**

Meditation: Extraordinary accomplishment often appears to be the work of strictly genius; however, we all contain our own unique genius within us. Success occurs when we express our individual brilliance and go the extra mile in pursuit of our goals. The secret is not to quit until you succeed. This is difficult work but gratifying in the end. Do not doubt or discard the reality and existence of your inner genius, simply trust and you will reveal the evidence of its force that resides within your soul.

Ask Yourself: What is your inner genius? How will you begin to express this genius today and not give up until you reach your desired goals?

I Affirm: Today, I will explore and trust my inner genius in all aspects of my daily journey.

JANUARY 7 *"There are no simple or easy formulas. In handling all life's experiences, we must endure a degree of emptiness and the agony of not knowing."*
— **M. Scott Peck**

Meditation: As we all have experienced, life is difficult at times, however, it is never necessary to give up. The goal is to put one foot in front of the other during these arduous times and remember that these feelings will soon pass. These difficulties will soon be resolved. Recognize and honor the emotions and move on. These difficult and emotional times will keep you full of gratitude for the enjoyable experiences to come. Keep pushing forward no matter what happens along the path. Difficulties are the factors that build you up and prepare you for success.

Ask Yourself: What can you learn from your emotional difficulties today? What are you grateful for at this point in your life? (Remember, put one foot in front of the other and these times will soon pass.)

I Affirm: Today, I will treat all my difficulties as opportunities for growth and enlightenment.

JANUARY 8 *"Spirituality is the attempt to be in harmony with the unseen order of things."*
— **William James**

Meditation: Life lacks structure, meaning, purpose, and peace without a connection to the omnipotent force that surrounds us. Be still and you will experience this power; have faith and this power will guide you. Connect with this force and find tranquility in this enlightening aspect of the Universe. It is not necessary for you to definitively understand this creative energy because it is beyond a human's capacity for comprehension. Just know it is always present and have faith that it is there to unite with you on your journey toward prosperity.

Ask Yourself: How will you embrace this unseen power today and allow it to guide you along life's illuminating journey?

I Affirm: Today, I will align with the powerful force of the Universe and allow it to gently guide me along my daily journey.

JANUARY **9**   *"Man is what he believes."*

— Anton Chekov

Meditation: Make a commitment today to believe in yourself. You are truly a unique individual in this world and have the ability to create the life you desire. Believe in yourself and the Universe will reward you with success. Belief and realization starts within you, then quickly externalizes to the life around you. If you believe, anything is possible and the amazing thing about belief is that it joins forces with reality and offers you all that you require to bring your belief into fruition.

Ask Yourself: How will you strive to believe in yourself today and manifest who you truly are?

I Affirm: Today, I will believe in my capacity to achieve greatness and become the human being that I desire to be.

⋆⟩━━◗ ◖━━⟨⋆

JANUARY **10** *"Money often costs too much."*

— Ralph Waldo Emerson

Meditation: Of course we need money to live, but is money as important as we make it out to be? Is it more important than spending time with your loved ones, enjoying a spectacular day in nature, or being present with your children to offer your love and compassion? There is often excessive emphasis put on the dollar and additional material possessions. Subsequently, there is not enough emphasis put on the genuine aspects in our life. Be honest with yourself and contemplate the valuable things in your life; money is probably not that prominent on your list.

Ask Yourself: Make a commitment not to overemphasize money or idolize material possessions today. Reflect upon the truly important things in your life. What will you do today that is genuinely important to your soul and separate from business and your normal monetary and material thoughts?

I Affirm: Today, I will focus on the spirit -filled aspects of my life rather than money, property, and prestige.

JANUARY **11** *"And if not now…when?"*

— Hillel

Meditation: We often express our plan to make important changes in our life in order to be happy, peaceful, more successful, and on and on. Although, our plans are usually to accomplish these things sometime in the future when, of course it is a better time. The issue with this is that life is only made up of present moments, thus if we always plan to change in the future, our life will be over before we make this commitment. Stop procrastinating and start making changes at this moment and begin to feel the benefits now rather than later.

Ask Yourself: What will you do to change and make improvements in your life RIGHT NOW?

I Affirm: Today, I will not postpone my dreams and aspirations; I will begin making them come true.

JANUARY **12** *"Its better that you live a week or two as a realized, free, totally serene loving human being than 90 years in the mayhem of the ego."*

— Stuart Wilde

Meditation: Our ego causes suffering in our lives and has one goal, which is to separate us from other human beings. The ego's continuous delusions detaches us from the true reality of our spirit. To live without the interference of the ego is a key to a fulfiling life as the spiritual beings we were destined to be. It is vital to slowly detach from the ego if you desire to live according to your spirit and fulfill your destined purpose for being here on earth.

Ask Yourself: Today, how will you completely surrender yourself to the moment and realize your true spiritual being?

I Affirm: Today, I will remain focused on the voice of my spirit rather than the demands of my ego.

JANUARY **13** *"Who dares nothing, need hope for nothing."*

— Johann von Schiller

Meditation: Life is a series of tests, challenges, and difficulties that we must work diligently at getting through on a daily basis in order to fulfill the purpose we are here for. If we give up or take the effortless path, we will never reach the potential that resides within us. We must risk, we must dare, and it is imperative that we make life adventurous. If nothing is risked in life, nothing remarkable will ever be accomplished.

Ask Yourself: How will you dare to live an adventurous and growth filled life today?

I Affirm: Today, I will look at everything that enters my path as an opportunity for growth and adventure.

JANUARY **14** *"One of the secrets of life is to make stepping stones out of stumbling blocks."*

— Jack Penn

Meditation: We often look at challenges in life as negative obstacles in our path to success; however, in reality, they are opportunities for personal and spiritual growth in order to lead us to our divine purpose and authentic life. We can choose to believe that challenges are a negative element upon our journey or learn to see them as opportunities for an elevated more meaningful life. Without challenges and difficulties in life, growth and evolution are impossible, thus life would be stagnant and tedious.

Ask Yourself: How will you turn difficulties and challenges into pertinent learning experiences today?

I Affirm: Today, I will search for significant learning experiences in each challenge that appears before me.

JANUARY **15** *"When you do one thing do it with all your might. Put your whole soul into it. Stamp it with your personality. Be active, be energetic, be enthusiastic and faithful, and you will accomplish your object."*

— **Ralph Waldo Emerson**

Meditation: Anything you do with your heart will be a triumphant victory. Be sure not to waste time and energy in your life doing anything with half the effort and no passion. Life is a masterpiece waiting to be created and you will not reach your potential without putting the energy of your heart and soul into every aspect of your artwork. Escape mediocrity and the so-called "normal" and release the excellence that is looming within you. It yearns to come out, but it must be summoned by you.

Ask Yourself: Find a project to work on and put all your energy into it today. What do you have intense passion for today that you can put all your energy into? (This will bring you the desired success you have been searching for; it all starts with your heart and soul and the energy you utilize. Excellence can be obtained in any aspect of your life with these two ingredients.)

I Affirm: Today, I will put my heart and soul into everything that I do; I will release the passion that has been hidden within me.

JANUARY **16** *"The future depends on what we do in the present."*

— **M. K. Gandhi**

Meditation: What you do in each moment ultimately adds up to be your future. Thus, there is no reason to worry or fret about the future because you have complete control of each moment you live today. Create the best moments you can and your future will consist of what you desire. Discontinue your habitual need to pollute the present with regret and guilt from the past and constant worries about the future. Center yourself and exude excellence in the now and the future you desire will take care of itself.

Ask Yourself: What will you do today in order to create a better future for you and your loved ones? How will you focus entirely upon the present?

I Affirm: Today, I will focus all of my thoughts and energy on the present moment.

JANUARY **17** *"True affluence is not needing anything."*

— Gary Snyder

Meditation: Our ego often saturates our life with unnecessary desires for the purpose of a single moment of sensory pleasure. Assess your true needs and you will discover that a majority of your possessions are merely drowning you. Remember, we are human beings not human "buyings." We are on this earth to "BE," not to "BUY." You will never buy your way into peace and serenity, but you can live your way into this if you choose the proper path. The path of peace and genuine happiness consists of being guided by your higher-self and detaching from your hedonistic ego's demands.

Ask Yourself: What does your soul want today? Quiet your ego and listen to the essence of your being, it is much more truthful and genuine.

I Affirm: Today, I will be mindful of the pure essence of my being and not be lead astray by my deluded ego.

JANUARY **18** *"Fall seven times, stand up eight."*

— Japanese Proverb

Meditation: Life consists of continuous experiences that help us to develop and discover who we truly are. Life knocks us down and our job is to get back up and grow from these experiences. Falling down is the only way we truly learn to walk and eventually run. Success depends on this constant perseverance and viewing difficulties as a positive experience rather than relying on our faulty past learning of failure as a negative experience. How you look at life is truly what matters.

Ask Yourself: How will you persevere today despite all the challenges that confront you? This habit of perseverance and turning difficulties into opportunities will help you to create the life you desire.

I Affirm: Today, I will practice perseverance and transform all difficulties into unique learning experiences.

JANUARY **19** *"Success comes in CANS, not CAN'TS."*

— Author Unknown

Meditation: The best thing that you can do from TODAY forward in your life is to eliminate the word "CAN'T" from your vocabulary when it comes to things you desire to do. If you feel the overwhelming urge to use "can't," then use it to ask yourself, "Why can't I?" rather than I can't." It is not that you can't do something, it's that you won't. Begin to believe that you can do anything you desire and do not allow yourself or anyone else to convince you differently. Finally put an end to this destructive semantic error and only tell yourself you CAN accomplish whatever you want as long as you apply determination and persistence in your efforts.

Ask Yourself: What can you do TODAY that you once told yourself you can't? Begin to do this in small increments and you will succeed. Most importantly, Can't is no longer part of your vocabulary from this moment on.

I Affirm: Today, I will tell myself what I can do and will do, rather than living with self-created limitations.

JANUARY **20** *"The heart has eyes that the brain knows nothing of."*

— Charles Parkhurst

Meditation: Our heart genuinely knows our spiritual destiny and it notices the signs presented to us by the Universe. Follow your heart and you will fulfill your life's purpose and prepare your self for eternity. You are an infinite being that is guided by spiritual energy; clasp hands with your guide and bask in the illumination of life.

Ask Yourself: How will you follow your hearts directions today rather than relying on your analytical ego?

I Affirm: Today, I will seek guidance from my heart and join hands with the energy of the Universe.

JANUARY **21** *"The best way to cheer yourself up is to try to cheer someone else up."*

— Mark Twain

Meditation: We often enter our inner realm and focus on everything negative about ourselves, about our lives, and about the world around us. This surely leads to despair and misplaced negative energy that hinders your experience of living. When feeling this way get out of yourself and help another member of your race, the HUMAN RACE that is. Fulfill the ultimate purpose and responsibility of human beings; lend your hand and your heart to a fellow human being in need.

Ask Yourself: Who will you help today? How will you offer yourself to this suffering individual today?

I Affirm: Today, I will offer my compassion and love to anyone who needs it.

JANUARY **22** *"There are no shortcuts to any place worth going."*

— Beverly Sills

Meditation: Personal growth and success are created by moving through all challenges and obstacles that are presented to us. Anything rewarding in your life will have numerous difficulties that will test your desire along the journey. If your desire is intense enough and your perseverance strong enough you will be rewarded beyond your imagination. Don't choose the simple path; face all the obstacles and barriers on the way and you will give birth to the creative and courageous being that is patiently waiting within you.

Ask Yourself: Will you search for shortcuts today or will you face life head on and be actively involved in your growth and evolution as a human being?

I Affirm: Today, I will face all obstacles head on and have faith in my ability to succeed.

JANUARY 23 *"Never give up then, for that is just the place, and time that the tide will turn."*

— **Harriet Beecher Stow**

Meditation: Success often comes when we least expect it. If you continue to forge ahead and persist through the struggle, through the defeats, and through the pain of the journey you will come out on the other side successful. This is tough work, but there are no great feats completed in this world without sacrifice and dedication. The miracle of success will wait and make you earn the reward, so prove that you are deserving of it by seeing the challenge to the end and never giving up, especially too soon.

Ask Yourself: How will you reframe your idea of a problem into what it truly is—a test?

I Affirm: Today, I will paint a clear picture in my mind of the success I will achieve through dedication and persistence.

JANUARY 24 *"It is reasonable to have perfection in our eye that we may always advance toward it, though we know it can never be reached."*

— **Samuel Johnson**

Meditation: Today, strive for progress in everything you do and give yourself credit for the great effort, rather than striving for perfection and criticizing yourself for not reaching the unreachable. The struggle to be perfect often takes an enormous amount of time out of our life and prevents us from doing what we were sent here to do. Your life is a work in progress and the journey is what makes you who you are. Strive for excellence in all that you do and that is perfection.

Ask Yourself: Today, just make progress. How will you focus on your life as a work in progress today and not seek perfection in everything you do?

I Affirm: Today, I will remind myself that I am human and was programmed to make mistakes in order to evolve.

JANUARY **25** *"Tension is a habit, relaxation is a habit. Bad habits can be broken, good habits formed."*

— **William James**

Meditation: Habits are formed by successive behaviors. We possess a variety of good habits and bad habits. Bad habits can easily be changed by simply practicing good habits on a daily basis. Success and growth in life come with the transformation of our low-energy habits into high-energy habits. Align with higher vibrations on a daily basis and you will see the results manifest in your life. Eventually, your good habits will be second nature.

Ask Yourself: What good habit are you going to embark on today?

I Affirm: Today, I will substitute one healthy behavior for an unhealthy behavior in order to begin cultivating a new good habit.

JANUARY **26** *"You cannot be anything if you want to be everything."*

— **Solomon Schechter**

Meditation: One of the most relevant facts in life is to realize that no matter how much you know, it's only a minute percentage of the knowledge available in the Universe. Today, live according to the specific purpose that inhabits your being. You were created to add a specific piece to the puzzle of the Universe. Concentrate on your piece today.

Ask Yourself: What is your purpose in life and how will you concentrate on this today?

I Affirm: Today, I will focus on the purpose that burns within my soul.

JANUARY **27** *"Be not simply good, be good for something."*

— Henry David Thoreau

Meditation: Human beings are given life with all its amenities and I believe we need to give something back to the world to use for further evolution. It is not our purpose to simply walk the earth, work at a mediocre job we despise, pay the bills, and then lay down and die. There is an ultimate purpose to pursue and this is what will create meaning in your life. Discover and embrace the passion that lies within your being, waiting to be realized. The passion is there, you may just need to clean some of the debris that is covering it and preventing its detection.

Ask Yourself: What will you leave the world as your personal gift?

I Affirm: Today, I will concentrate on my unique passion and reflect upon what I can give to the Universe.

JANUARY **28** *"Great minds have purposes, others have wishes."*

— Washington Irving

Meditation: Life can be extremely lonely and appear meaningless without pursuing your authentic and innate purpose. We are all born with a purpose, it is our job to cultivate it and make it materialize in our life. Your spirit will lead in this cultivation and you will be given the clues to what this purpose may be. It is your job to acknowledge your purpose, accept it, and work diligently with passionate determination in order to manifest it in your life. This is how success is born.

Ask Yourself: What is your purpose and are you working at this on a daily basis?

I Affirm: Today, I will set aside some time and write a few pages concerning my purpose and mission in life.

JANUARY **29** *"For true success ask yourself these four questions: why?; why not?; why not me?; Why not now?"*

— James Allen

Meditation: Success is rather simple if you rid yourself of all the negative energy that has been built up inside you for years. Stop doubting and start believing, stop criticizing and start commending, stop worrying and start acting, and stop procrastinating and start achieving. All of this is within your reach if you only believe in your purpose and your worthiness as a unique, special, and capable human being.

Ask Yourself: How will you begin achieving your goals by utilizing the above questions today?

I Affirm: Today, I will believe in myself completely and begin confidently working toward the goals I desire in my life.

JANUARY **30** *"A prejudice is a vagrant opinion without visible means of support."*

— Ambrose Bierce

Meditation: Do not continue living this precious life through ignorance. It is our responsibility to gather knowledge concerning every aspect of life prior to making any judgments. Gain knowledge and allow yourself to live a non-judgmental existence based on truth rather than unfounded bias caused by fear. Leave the prejudice and ignorance behind and you will know peace. Differentiate yourself from societal judgments and opinions founded upon ignorance.

Ask Yourself: What or who do you make judgments about without adequate knowledge? Are you willing to gain knowledge today and leave the judgments behind?

I Affirm: Today, I will clear my mind of judgments and ignorance and live life according to truth.

JANUARY **31** *"The ultimate measure of a man is not where he stands in moments of comfort and convenience, but where he stands in times of challenge and controversy."*
— **Dr. Martin Luther King, Jr.**

Meditation: Meaning in life is derived from adversities and challenges along your journey. This defines who you are and what you are willing to do to pursue your destined purpose and passions in life. To persist and stand strong for what you believe and what you are pursuing is what sets apart those who achieve excellence and those who remain in the comfortable conformity of life. You can choose courage and dedication to succeed in your life or you can conform and be haunted by regrets and misgivings of challenges not undertaken.

Ask Yourself: How will you meet the challenge of the day in an enlightened way?

I Affirm: Today, I will face life with vigor and enthusiasm and not back down from any challenge.

FEBRUARY 1 *"It is not the length of life, but depth of life."*

— Ralph Waldo Emerson

Meditation: Forget about the past and don't worry about the future, just live deeply today. Today and right now is all that life truly consists of. If you are not experiencing the present moment, you are allowing life to pass you by. Envelope yourself in the now and experience the peace and serenity of living mindfully. Stop allowing life to pass you by and rejoice in it today. I believe this is where we will find genuine happiness, this is the secret of life; living in the moment is the key to your success and tranquility that you have been searching external sources for way too long.

Ask Yourself: What do you get out of living in the past and future?

I Affirm: Today, I will fully live in the now and embrace the gift of life at this very moment.

FEBRUARY 2 *"Don't be discouraged, it's often the last key in the bunch that opens the lock."*

— Author Unknown

Meditation: Our life in this Universe consists of constant challenges, but that's simply all they are, challenges. Not failures, not mistakes, not errors, simply challenges to grow from spiritually. Accept the challenges, grow from them, and advance forward on your journey. The secret is not to give up before the miraculous manifests in your life. With persistence and undying determination, the miracle of success will appear when you are least expecting it.

Ask Yourself: How will you reconsider discouragement today and utilize these times for spiritual growth?

I Affirm: Today, I will see challenges in a new light and search for the growing experience in every situation.

FEBRUARY 3 *"When angry count to ten before you speak, if very angry, one hundred."*

— **Thomas Jefferson**

Meditation: Immense guilt, shame, and regret are often produced when we resort to acting out our anger in an impulsive fashion. Make it a point and a goal today to count to ten or a hundred or even a thousand when feeling angry. This little exercise will save you a lot of time and emotional energy in the long run. Anger will pass if dealt with effectively and you can remain guilt, shame, and regret free. It is not bad to feel angry. What can result in bad consequences is how you handle your anger. Keep in mind that holding on to anger or acting out inappropriately only harms you and does nothing to the person, situation, or institution that you have anger towards.

Ask Yourself: Can you make a commitment today to deal with anger as discussed by Mr. Jefferson? Do you think it will help you in your daily living? Does anger help you live effectively and serenely? Does anger have any helpful attributes in obtaining your goals?

I Affirm: Today, I will not allow anger to ruin my day; if I feel angry I will deal with it in a healthy manner.

FEBRUARY 4 *"I have a dream…"*

— **Dr. Martin Luther King, Jr.**

Meditation: There is no difference between you and this remarkable man. He courageously took a risk to express his beliefs. This one man had a dream, was able to articulate it, and began making it happen. This proves how much one person can do in life if they are strong, courageous, and persistent. This man acknowledged his true purpose in life and lived it. What a risk! This will produce genuine success and true happiness if modeled in your own life.

Ask Yourself: What is your dream and how can you initiate its manifestation in the world?

I Affirm: Today, I will live according to my heart and be the human being that I know I can be.

FEBRUARY **5** *"Advice is seldom welcome, and those who need it the most, like it the least."*

— Lord Chesterfield

Meditation: If success is what you desire, it is imperative to keep an open mind and be willing to listen to those attempting to impart information to you. We often desire to quickly reject information; however, growth is stunted when we take this route. Listen to what is being said, contemplate it, internalize it, then, if it doesn't fit, you may simply let it go. Never take the chance of prematurely discarding knowledge and wisdom that may guide you on your path to success in life. Always refrain from thinking that you know everything and that what you believe is the absolute truth. These mistakes can prevent you from growth and block you from success.

Ask Yourself: Can you be open to new information today? Can you ask someone for help?

I Affirm: Today, I will seek novel learning experiences and listen to the silent wisdom of the universal consciousness.

FEBRUARY **6** *"Success is not measured by what a man accomplishes, but by the opposition he has encountered, and the courage with which he has maintained the struggle against overwhelming odds."*

— Charles Lindbergh

Meditation: Anything worthwhile in life will always present you with struggles and challenges. Your job is to face these times with courage and persistence and continue traveling your path with zealous determination. Remember that your spirit will take over when your mind has had enough. Greatness occurs beyond the mind and in the presence of your soul. Use adversities as the critical building blocks to your success. These blocks will provide you with an infallible foundation to build your life upon.

Ask Yourself: Can you allow your spirit to guide you today and get you through the struggles present in your life? Do you trust your spirit in these times of need?

I Affirm: Today, I will tap into the strength of my spirit and allow it to lead me in my daily journey.

FEBRUARY **7** *"A year from now you may wish you started from today."*

— **Karen Lamb**

Meditation: We often reminisce about our past and regret the things we did not accomplish that were passions and dreams belonging to us. We answer this regret with, "Well, it is too late now; I'll just get over it." Nevertheless, do you ever get over not fulfilling your innate desires and purpose? It is never too late to accomplish your dreams and fantasies. They need to be initiated right now without turning back. You owe this to yourself and the world. Get to work and begin creating what you truly desire. This is what life is all about; don't let it slip away again because you may not have the opportunity to pursue your dreams again in the future.

Ask Yourself: What life-long dream or goal will you take the first step toward today?

I Affirm: Today, I will act upon one of my burning desires.

FEBRUARY **8** *"Let every man be respected as an individual and no man idolized."*

— **Albert Einstein**

Meditation: The idea of inferiority and superiority is the great delusion of the world. We think of ourselves as either better or worse than all other human beings. This is probably one of the most destructive ideas that man has created. Is it possible to worship another human being just like ourselves? In addition, is it right to degrade another human being just like ourselves? When we begin to grasp reality and the absolute truth of humanity, we will begin to succeed in manifesting peace and unity in the world.

Ask Yourself: Why is the concept of human equality so hard to understand? Do you entertain and often believe that you are better or worse than other human beings? What is this based on?

I Affirm: Today, I will look closely at the truth of humanity and attempt to see myself in all human beings.

FEBRUARY **9** *"Our lives begin to end the day we become silent about things that matter."*

— Dr. Martin Luther King, Jr.

Meditation: Our spirit pulls us toward genuine truth and empowering beliefs. If you believe in something with all your heart and soul, do not allow society to drag you into its illusion. Remain spiritually alive and always seek truth within your higher-self, not your ego. Live this truth and fight for your beliefs. This is what we were brought here to do. Hang on, live your beliefs in the face of adversity, and never back down. The majority or the popular opinion does not define truth; it is defined within your heart and soul.

Ask Yourself: What do you personally believe that society attempts to oppose?

I Affirm: Today, I will not allow societies beliefs to interfere with my true heart-felt beliefs.

FEBRUARY **10** *"The secret of success is constancy to purpose."*

— Benjamin Disraeli

Meditation: Be diligent in your pursuit of excellence; be assured if you are aligned with your ultimate purpose you will be rewarded with everlasting success in all arenas of your life. The success of the soul is beyond any experience you have had or will ever have in your life. Be prepared for a life beyond your imagination if you diligently and persistently pursue your passions. Do not allow any obstacles or challenges to slow you down; continue to learn and grow from each situation and remain on your path to personal and spiritual victory.

Ask Yourself: Are you aligned with your ultimate purpose today and are you committed to fulfiling this purpose no matter what stands in your way?

I Affirm: Today, I will strive to live my purpose with vibrancy and undying enthusiasm.

FEBRUARY **11**   *"The good and the wise lead quiet lives."*

— Euripides

Meditation: You will know when you are on the correct path in your life when you no longer join in with the chaos and noise of society and are able to follow your inner guidance without doubts and fears. The demands of your ego will become softer and eventually silent. Your true self will take over and you will come to see through the illusion of worldly demands, resulting in the ability to live with meaning and purpose on a daily basis. Lead a life of strength, purpose, meaning, and silent passion today. This is the genuine passageway to a successful and peace filled life.

Ask Yourself: How will you silence your mind today in order to live according to your soul?

I Affirm: Today, I will listen intently to the whispers of my soul and gently escape the negativity of my ego.

FEBRUARY **12**   *"Know your limits but never stop trying to exceed them."*

— Author Unknown

Meditation: Limits and self-imposed restrictions come from a place of fear. As a genuine spiritual being, there are truly only the limits your ego creates. Destroy those limits and exceed them. Open your mind and delve into your imagination in order to break through the walls of your ego and the boundaries of society. Limits are self-created and can always be redefined. Face the fear of the unknown and continue to overthrow the restrictions that surround you. This will allow you to reach your innate potential and discover the endless possibilities that avail themselves in the Universe.

Ask Yourself: How will you demonstrate to your ego today that your spirit will set the limits rather than your mind?

I Affirm: Today, I will explore my inner world and allow my spiritual being to define what my limits are.

FEBRUARY **13**   *"Reading is to the mind what exercise is to the body."*

— Joseph Addison

Meditation: Reading is our link to the combined wisdom and knowledge of the universal consciousness. We can amazingly have a dialogue with Einstein, Freud, Jung, Emerson, Thoreau, and countless other great minds of the past and present. Read and discover the world like never before. To continuously seek knowledge and truth through books is an act that all should pursue.

Ask Yourself: Are you keeping up on the suggested monthly readings? Is it guiding you to your higher purpose and potential?

I Affirm: Today, I will make a commitment to begin seeking knowledge from the wisdom contained in great works of written expression.

FEBRUARY **14**   *"Make a personal decision to be in love with the most beautiful, exciting, worthy person ever—you."*

— Dr. Wayne Dyer

Meditation: Love is a precious gift that you must first give yourself. Embrace the uniqueness of your being and begin to engage passionately in the admiration of your whole self. You have a specific meaning and purpose for being alive, thus it is your responsibility to honor your life. Before you can engage in any other intimate relationship in your life, you must devote love and respect for every aspect of your being.

Ask Yourself: How will you express your personal love today?

I Affirm: Today, I will treat myself with loving kindness and appreciate each unique characteristic that makes me, me.

FEBRUARY **15**   *"Life is a school: why not try taking the curriculum?"*
— Proverb

Meditation: Enroll today and begin your studies in Life 101. See everything as a lesson today leading to spiritual growth and be sure not to give up on this eternal curriculum. There will be no grades, only lessons and opportunities for personal and spiritual growth. Do your best in class and learn each day from every lesson, challenge, and difficulty that comes along in your journey. Remain conscious of the fact that everything is an educational experience, so give it your best and never resign from your mission toward successful living.

Ask Yourself: Will you enroll today as a new student and say hello to your professor, the Universe?

I Affirm: Today, I will see everyone and every situation in my life as an essential part of my learning process.

FEBRUARY **16**   *"Emotions are like waves. Watch them come and go on the vast ocean of existence."*
— Proverb

Meditation: At times, it may appear that your negative emotions are never going to end. Be assured that these emotions like all other states of mind will pass. Begin to allow yourself to honor all emotions, learn from them, embrace them, then allow them to pass like the waves of the sea. See them come in, heed their intended lesson, then let them pass by calmly. Emotions merely act as guides in your journey. No emotions are bad, wrong or should be judged in any way. Feel them, do not attach to them, and allow them to steadily flow like a serene stream in the middle of the woods.

Ask Yourself: How will you effectively handle difficult emotions today?

I Affirm: Today, I will allow emotions to simply be emotions and not give them control of my being.

FEBRUARY 17

> *"The only thing you will take through these pearly gates is what you've given away."*
> — **Marcia Moore**

Meditation: Allow kindness and compassion to emanate from your being today. Allow the world to feel your love for humankind, experience the gift of your soul, and benefit from your altruistic and benevolent nature. You are a powerful human being and can greatly affect others lives simply by offering a kind word, a kind act, or just a smile. Get to work on the most important aspect of your life; what you can give to the world rather than concentrating on what you can receive. Give something to humanity today and rejoice in the power of this sacred act.

Ask Yourself: What will you give of yourself today and whom will you give this to? Remember, giving from the heart and the soul doesn't have to mean material or monetary giving. Gifts from the heart and soul have much more value and power than material offerings.

I Affirm: Today, I will genuinely and selflessly offer my compassion for the benefit of humanity.

FEBRUARY 18

> *"Let us be silent, that we may hear the whispers of the Gods."*
> — **Ralph Waldo Emerson**

Meditation: Silencing the ego allows our eternal voice to be expressed and heard. Stop for a moment and take a break from the chaos and delusion of the ego. Allow your spiritual voice to whisper in your ear and be heard. This is the secret of remaining on your path to genuine success and peace. If you stop and silence your mind, you will surely hear the powerful voice of your soul. Slow down and enjoy the truth and beauty of your spirit. It will guide you to peace in a world full of noise.

Ask Yourself: Do you have time today to listen to your higher voice? What is it telling you?

I Affirm: Today, I will pay attention to the whispers of my soul.

FEBRUARY **19** *"Remember no human condition is ever permanent. Then you will not be overjoyed in good fortune or too sorrowful in your misfortune."*

— Socrates

Meditation: Allow yourself to create and experience balance in your life rather than the uncomfortable roller coaster of emotions that you often travel on. Extremes always create the emotional high or emotional low that takes precious energy from your life. Balanced living is the secret to peace and tranquility without always being at either end of the pole. Walk today in the balance and harmony of the Universe rather than the extremes of the ego.

Ask Yourself: What do you need to do to balance your inner life today?

I Affirm: Today, I will travel along the harmonic road of the Universe rather than being caught in the chaotic traffic of worldly illusions.

FEBRUARY **20** *"He who laughs, lasts."*

— Proverb

Meditation: Humor is one of the most effective coping skills you can take advantage of in your life. To be able to laugh at life and yourself is a gift that can make your journey much more satisfying and allow you to experience life in a relaxed and less grim manner. It is often said that it takes many more muscles in your face to frown than it does to smile. Lighten up and remember that you are an infinite being, therefore, you have eternity to do whatever it is you believe is such a crisis or emergency in your life. Begin to laugh at yourself and the challenges that the Universe places before you. Life really isn't that serious, so stop making it appear that way and have a little fun.

Ask Yourself: How will you take your daily dose of humor and add some fun to your life today?

I Affirm: Today, I will remind myself that life isn't as serious as my mind makes it out to be.

FEBRUARY **21**

"Let me walk three weeks in the footsteps of my enemy, carry the same burden, have the same trials as he, before I say one word to criticize."
— **An Indian Chief 's Prayer**

Meditation: One of the most remarkable qualities accessible to us as human beings is our unique ability to empathize with one another. It is a phenomenal experience to enter another's inner world and recognize that they have pain, despair, struggles, and feelings much like our own. Remember, we are connected to all things and all beings in this Universe, so when you get upset or annoyed with another human being, remind yourself that they may just be having a painful day. Accept them rather than judging them. Help them rather than condemning them. Have compassion and empathy for all you come in contact with and your life will not be the same and neither will there's.

Ask Yourself: How will you demonstrate your ability to empathize with other human beings today?

I Affirm: Today, I will attempt to enter the inner world of other human beings in my life and realize that they may be in need of some genuine compassion.

FEBRUARY **22**

"Our life is frittered away by detail…simply, simplify."
— **Henry David Thoreau**

Meditation: Our analytical mind often takes away the beauty of life by over-complicating everything in its path. This may make us feel intellectual, in control, powerful, and superior, but it also does one other important thing; it takes away the essence of life and our ability to be in tune with our innate spiritual beings. Spirituality is not analyzed, defined, or created in the intellect; spirituality is a simple feeling that we must allow ourselves to experience and feel rather than characterize within our mind. Stop thinking so obsessively today and allow your spirit to breathe.

Ask Yourself: How can you give your analytical self a break today and allow your spirit to enjoy life right in this very moment?

I Affirm: Today, I will Stop thinking so obsessively and allow my spirit to breathe.

FEBRUARY 23   *"Happiness depends upon ourselves."*

— Aristotle

Meditation: Step out of the delusion of the ego that tempts you to believe that happiness is found in an external event, person, or thing. Happiness will eternally be a choice that human beings have the ability to make. Many individuals spend a majority of their lives searching for happiness outside themselves and, unfortunately, do not find it in temporary sensory pleasures. The earlier in your life you accept this, the quicker you can move on and experience the true happiness and contentment that is abundantly available in life.

Ask Yourself: Will you choose happiness today or continue your wild pursuit for pleasure in the material world?

I Affirm: Today, I will open the doorway of my soul and tap into the happiness and abundance that exists within.

FEBRUARY 24   *"Most folks are about as happy as they make up their minds to be."*

— Abraham Lincoln

Meditation: The secret to happiness is making a decision to be happy in this very moment. If you strive to be happy every moment of your life, you are sure to live a blissful existence. Life consists of this moment right now; this is all you have control over. Make that important decision to be happy in the moment today and you are sure to have a fulfiling day that will bring much contentment and peace along your journey.

Ask Yourself: What will it take for you to make a decision to be happy in the moment today?

I Affirm: Today, I will embrace the present and discard the illusions of the past and future; I will remind myself that right now is all that life is truly made of.

February

FEBRUARY **25**   *"Rest the sweet sauce of labor."*

— **Plutarch**

Meditation: Relax and reward yourself with silence today and withdraw from the turmoil of the world. Honor the hard work you do everyday and give yourself a well-deserved retreat from the clamor of life. Allow your mind, body, and soul to feel the healing energy of the universal force. Work and chaos will be there for you to contend with tomorrow and, actually, when you depart this material world, there will still be tasks remaining on your "To-Do" list . Take a break and embrace the silence of your spirit and absorb the consoling and tranquil energy of the Universe.

Ask Yourself: How will you treat yourself to the solitude of the moment and take a necessary break from chaos today?

I Affirm: Today, I will relax and allow the power of the present moment to heal my entire being.

FEBRUARY **26**   *"No person was ever honored for what he received. Honor has been the reward for what he gave."*
— **Calvin Coolidge**

Meditation: Individuals who have been honored throughout history are those who did not seek or crave honor, but lived a purposeful and passionate life devoted to benefiting humanity. Honor is given to those who give their lives to a worthy cause and leave something for the world's benefit. Truly honorable human beings never expect anything in return for their gifts to humanity. The real reward is the genuine happiness and peace that is received within.

Ask Yourself: How will you align with your ultimate purpose today and give to humanity without expecting anything in return? Giving can be as simple as helping someone across the street, opening a door for someone, or just offering your ear to listen to someone struggling with life.

I Affirm: Today, I will offer a genuine and selfless gift to humanity overflowing with the passion contained within my heart and soul.

FEBRUARY 27   *"Out of suffering have emerged the strongest souls."*

— Edwin Chapin

Meditation: Suffering is a requirement for personal growth and spiritual evolution. Embrace and honor the challenges and difficulties presented to you on your journey, these are what will ultimately create the spiritual being you are destined to become. Invite these challenges, pay tribute to them, travel through them with determination, and celebrate the unique being that you are becoming. Be certain not to allow suffering and adversity to get you down, but use it to your advantage at every opportunity you are given. Remind yourself to learn a lesson from every challenge on your journey.

Ask Yourself: How will you honor and embrace your challenges today?

I Affirm: Today, I will search for the vital learning experience in every moment of my daily passage.

FEBRUARY 28   *"Great men are they who see that the spiritual is stronger than any material force."*
— Ralph Waldo Emerson

Meditation: Escape the illusion of the material world and initiate your life of meaning and purpose in the spiritual world. Embrace the spirit within you and enjoy a worthy and serene existence. Suffering will disappear after you recognize that the material is temporary and detach from this binding power. Spirituality is genuine and will provide you with the tranquility and peace that you have been searching for in external pleasures.

Ask Yourself: How will you begin your detachment from the material world and tap into your innate spiritual being?

I Affirm: Today, I will tune into the omnipresent spiritual force that provides for all my needs rather than relying on fleeting material pleasures.

FEBRUARY **29**

"Try not to become a man (person) of success but rather try to become a man (person) of value."
— **Albert Einstein**

Meditation: Striving in life for the common societal and worldly definition of success leads us on the erroneous path and causes us to compromise our true inner selves. Endeavor to seek and discover your true spiritual path, which will lead to genuine success and contentment in life, as well as the fulfilment of your universal purpose. Give what you have to humanity and success will take care of itself. Step away from the great delusion of human thinking and liberate yourself from the common material and monetary obsessions.

Ask Yourself: How will you let go of society's definition of success and stay on your spiritual path today?

I Affirm: Today, I will define success in my own personal way and strive for success based on my criteria.

MARCH **1** *"The art of being wise is the art of knowing what to overlook."*
— **William James**

Meditation: Many lives are unnecessarily interrupted by paying close attention to irrelevant and insignificant aspects of life. We must learn to prioritize our lives and put what is truly of value above the inconsequential nonsense that we often focus on. Break out of your self imposed boundaries and do what your heart says, do what your soul desires, and the rest will fall into place.

Ask Yourself: What do you truly value and desire in your life?

I Affirm: Today, I will prioritize and focus on what is truly of value in my life.

MARCH **2** *"You are today where your thoughts have brought you; you will be tomorrow where your thoughts take you."*
— **James Allen**

Meditation: This is an ideal time to pose a question to your inner self: Are you Satisfied with who you are and where you are at in your life today? If your answer is yes, wonderful. Continue to create the thoughts that take you where you truly desire to be. If your answer is no and you desire to be someone and somewhere else, you need to change your thoughts and beliefs regarding your life. Your personal and spiritual transformation begins today. Keep in mind that your thoughts and your beliefs are the building blocks and foundation of what you materialize in your external world.

Ask Yourself: How will you change your thoughts and beliefs about life today?

I Affirm: Today, I will not allow my thoughts or beliefs to be influenced by the negativity of my ego.

MARCH 3   *"Children are our most valuable natural resource."*

— Herbert Hoover

Meditation: Begin to treat the children of the world as the creators of a new Universe. Teach them, love them, give them genuine knowledge, and visualize in them a transformed and improved world. They truly are what define the future and we must save them from the harsh delusions of society. One way to add purpose and meaning to your life is to make it a point to mentor and sculpt the children around you into leaders for a successful evolution of the world.

Ask Yourself: How will you aid in the survival and increased improvement of the future by giving something valuable to a child today?

I Affirm: Today, I will remember that I was once an innocent child seeking love and compassion in a chaotic world; I will give this love and compassion freely to a child in need.

MARCH 4   *"You will never change your life until you change something you do daily. The secret of your success is found in your daily routine."*

— John C. Maxwell

Meditation: Life, very simply consists of individual precious moments just like this one right now. These moments added together develop into days. This concept is very basic, yet profound. The secret of success is to do something each moment and each day that will revolutionize your life. Develop a positive daily routine to get you where you want to go. Put your goal or dream in writing and begin your journey through daily actions today. You will be pleasantly surprised with the results this simple modification will produce in your life.

Ask Yourself: What positive daily routine will you implement in your life beginning this very moment?

I Affirm: Today, I will initiate a simple yet positive change in my life and visualize the transformation that it will create.

MARCH **5**   *"If we change within, our outer life will change also."*

— **Jean Shinoda Bolen**

Meditation: When we begin to change our thoughts and beliefs and focus on our inner life, our external world begins to change around us. This is true because we begin to create our own reality and perception of life. We finally get on our individualized spiritual path and create the life we aspire to live. We are finally receptive enough and capable of seeing the clues the Universe Presents to us and are willing to follow the guidance of our soul. This only happens by diving inside and searching for our true self. To do this, you must break through the boundaries of the outside world.

Ask Yourself: How will you change yourself today in order to initiate improvement in your outer life?

I Affirm: Today, I will venture within and make the inner changes that are a necessity for my success.

MARCH **6**   *"Surely this must be an ancient Proverb: If the situation is killing you, get the hell out."*

— **Hugh Prather**

Meditation: Taking the necessary action and getting the hell out of a destructive situation appears to be very straightforward and pure common sense. However, each day around the world, human beings continue to remain in destructive situations and with destructive people. Getting the hell out all begins with having enough faith and belief in yourself as a worthwhile human being. Believing that you deserve something better and asking for the help you need will get you out and keep you out of harms way. You deserve to live a peaceful and happy life. I know this, but the goal is for you to come to believe this truth with all of your being.

Ask Yourself: How will you love yourself and believe in your worthiness as a human being today?

I Affirm: Today, I will assess my life and take action to get out of any harmful situation; I will remind myself that I am a unique worthy human being.

MARCH 7 *"Look deep, deep into nature, and then you will understand everything better."*

— Albert Einstein

Meditation: Look today at the perfection of a flower, a snowflake, the sky, or just of a blade of grass. This will surely illustrate the perfection of your creator. Just contemplate the transformation of human beings from one cell to a perfect harmony of countless systems. This is nothing short of miraculous and enlightening. Where does this all come from? What created this perfection in life? Is there a higher force in charge of the universal precision? If so, everything has this force and everything is connected. Find this connection and join in. This is where you will discover genuine serenity, peace, and happiness.

Ask Yourself: What are your thoughts on the perfection of the Universe and how can you use the power of your creator in your life today?

I Affirm: Today, I will remain mindful of the perfection of the Universe and everything that surrounds me.

MARCH 8 *"Nature does not hurry, yet everything is accomplished."*

— Lao Tzu

Meditation: Be patient today and allow the Universe to guide you. Eliminate the hurry and anxiety that pervades your life and allow yourself to feel the natural calm of your soul. Life was not created to be full of urgency, anxiety, hatred, fear, worry, and all the other detrimental energies that bombard us on a daily basis. Humans created this way of life; society continues to live this way and we just tag along. Come back to the natural course of the Universe and rejoice in the peace and tranquility of life. It is not necessary to take part in society's chaotic philosophy of reality.

Ask Yourself: How can you create peace in your daily life today?

I Affirm: Today, I will unite with the natural flow of the Universe and feel the harmony within my mind, body and soul.

MARCH **9** *"Ultimate happiness cannot be derived from sensual pleasures."*

— Mark Epstein, M.D.

Meditation: Endlessly, we pursue happiness without searching within ourselves. Your true self, your higher self, and your spirit are eternally blissful. They live in the euphoria of life. The quest is allowing this happiness within to escape the illusory life of the ego and material world. This is done by surrendering to your spirit and allowing it to guide you on your infinite journey of life. You can choose this now or wait until later in life, however, much suffering can be bypassed and much genuine pleasure can be enjoyed if you choose to escape the boundaries of your ego and the combined ego of the world.

Ask Yourself: Will you continue seeking pleasure outside yourself or will you begin to discover and unleash the happiness already residing within your being?

I Affirm: Today, I will recognize the happiness that resides within my being and stop relying on temporary external pleasures.

MARCH **10** *"Few things are impossible to diligence and skill…Great works are performed, not by strength, but by perseverance."*

— Samuel Johnson

Meditation: Today, when you feel like giving up on yourself or any aspect of your life, just endure a bit further. The Universe will provide you with strength and see you through. What creates greatness in this Universe is a human being's ability to continue walking when times get tough, to continue facing the challenges, and to continue growing and learning from the difficulties placed in front of us. The miraculous happens when you go beyond the physical potential of your being and access the unlimited potential of your spiritual nature.

Ask Yourself: What is your plan to persevere rather than stop short of success today?

I Affirm: Today, I will persist along my spiritual path regardless of the obstacles that attempt to obstruct my progress.

MARCH **11** *"Success is loving your work."*

— Liz Smith

Meditation: There is one thing for sure; if you have passion and zest for your work, you will be successful and rise to the top of whatever you do. Daily effort that correlates highly with your purpose in life lets you know that you are on the path created specifically for your unique soul. You have an innate purpose that you must discover in your life, which results in not "working" but living your ultimate purpose. This purpose becomes your life and transforms the way you exist. Find it and live it. This is your job that the Universe has hired you for.

Ask Yourself: Look at the work in your life today. Do you love your work or would you rather be doing something else? Do you feel passion and purpose in your work or have you settled for mediocrity?

I Affirm: Today, I will unleash the passion within my heart and endeavor to live a life of ultimate purpose.

◦◦═◎ ◎═◦◦

MARCH **12** *"All human wisdom is summed up in two words: wait and hope."*

— Alexander Dumas

Meditation: Be patient and allow the Universe to catch up with you today. The Universe desires nothing but true success for you. Remember, this is not material success but spiritual success. You will feel the difference when you allow the creative energy of your soul to guide you rather than conforming to the chaotic and egocentric approach of society. Take a deep breath and listen to the quiet voice of the Universe that surrounds you.

Ask Yourself: What will you do to be patient and hopeful today?

I Affirm: Today, I will participate in the calmness and serenity of the Universe rather than the noise and disarray of society.

MARCH **13** *"The world is a book, and those who do not travel, read only a page."*

— St. Augustine

Meditation: Life, the Universe, and the world, consist of infinite pages, eternal chapters, and inexhaustible "stories" of growth, triumph, and love. Plan to move forward on your reading adventure, get out, experience, see, love, dream, and succeed. Read the book of life intensely and create your tale of success. Take a voyage inside your being, into novel situations, into new cultures, and discover the connection of humanity and the oneness of the Universe.

Ask Yourself: What is the title of your next chapter?

I Affirm: Today, I will notice the sacred in all of life and honor the divinity of existence.

MARCH **14** *"If you do more than what you are paid to do you will eventually be paid more for what you do."*

— Zig Ziglar

Meditation: A periphery benefit of our jobs is certainly that we get paid, since we obviously need money to survive. Although, is that what it's all about? Is that our reason for living and working? I don't think so! We work the majority of our life for a paycheck, spend the money, and consistently do this over and over again. That doesn't sound accurate to me. The central reason for working is to release your unlimited potential as a human being and discover your purpose in this Universe. Your work is to do the very best and be the very best human being possible. In the meantime, give something to the world.

Ask Yourself: How can you add excellence, purpose, and meaning to your job today? If you do not have passion for your profession, follow the guidance of your spirit and it will direct you to your ultimate purpose and meaning in life.

I Affirm: Today, I will allow the guidance of my spirit to direct me towards my ultimate purpose in life.

MARCH 15 *"Put your future in good hands, your own."*

— Author Unknown

Meditation: Your inner self knows exactly where you need to go and what you need to do. Its ultimate purpose is to guide you on your journey through life in order to reach maximum fulfilment. Detach from the delusional self created by society and follow your inner compass in order to allow abundance and peace to flow freely into your life.

Ask Yourself: What is your plan to allow the guidance of your inner self to take over today?

I Affirm: Today, I will rely on the genius within me to set the course of my life.

MARCH 16 *"If you wish to change society, change yourself first."*

— Thomas Carlyle

Meditation: Think for a moment, are there are any benefits or productivity of criticism, complaining, and constantly judging society? Human beings exactly like you created society and have made it the way it is presently. Subsequently, this translates into the fact that by changing yourself and others following this example of self-change, society will change one person and one day at a time. This is the one and only industrious approach at producing changes in society. If we follow society and remain silent, nothing will change it will only deteriorate.

Ask Yourself: How will you work on changing yourself today in order to act as a catalyst for societal change?

I Affirm: Today, I will focus on what changes I need to make in order to help transform society a little at a time.

MARCH **17** *"Challenges are what make life interesting, overcoming them is what makes life meaningful."*
— **Joshua Marine**

Meditation: Success is awarded to the person who has no fear and bravely confronts challenges head on. The successful individual pursues their goal with passion and determination and never gives up no matter what happens throughout the journey. Challenges are what define a human being; you can either bow down and allow challenges to defeat you or you can stand up and distinguish yourself by your approach to overcoming and growing from these challenges. Surviving challenges and difficulties along your journey is mandatory for personal and spiritual evolution. Invite them, honor them, and embrace them as a vital part of your life. Without challenges, there is no development or advancement within humanity.

Ask Yourself: How will you approach challenges today in your life?

I Affirm: Today, I will face challenges head on and utilize them as instruments for personal and spiritual growth.

MARCH **18** *"A will finds a way."*
— **Orison Swett Marden**

Meditation: If you have discovered your purpose in life and the one thing that you have immense passion for, you will be a great success. Your spirit will point you in the right direction and you will conquer that which you desire. You will ascertain new ways to get you to where your true self desires to be, you will run, jump, leap, and triumph over any obstacle that gets in your way. Determination and persistence will be your allies and you will reach the peak of success. Remember this singleness of purpose is what you are here for and it is your job to fulfill it for the development of humanity and for the evolution of your soul.

Ask Yourself: Have you allowed yourself to recognize your dreams, your desires, and your goals that link you to your genuine purpose along this journey? If yes, what are they and what is your action plan? If not, why not and what is your plan for recognizing and pursuing your purpose in life?

I Affirm: Today, I will remember that I have a vital purpose in this Universe and that it is my responsibility to fulfill this obligation.

MARCH **19** *"Restlessness and discontent are the necessities of progress."*

— **Thomas Edison**

Meditation: To always live in perfect harmony is to not grow and evolve as a spiritual being. Without pain, suffering, challenges, and difficulties, the world would surely be a lifeless and stagnate place. These states of being are necessary for the growth of the person and the soul. Honor the difficult times and challenge yourself to grow spiritually each day. Growth is your purpose in this eternal journey; choose it now or later, but eventually you will be forced to deal with this truth.

Ask Yourself: How will you embrace the opportunities for growth in your life rather than allowing them to create disparaging energy within you?

I Affirm: Today, I will face adversity with passion and excitement while realizing that challenges are great opportunities for spiritual growth.

MARCH **20** *"Man is his own worst enemy."*

— **Cicero**

Meditation: We are often disturbed when another individual disrespects us, irritates us, annoys us, or criticizes us. Nevertheless, throughout each day we consistently engage in this same behavior against ourselves. Once we are able to discontinue this absurd behavior toward ourselves and gain respect for the worthiness of our being, it will not matter the least bit what another thinks about us, says about us, or the way they act toward us. We are what matters.

Ask Yourself: What will you do to show the utmost respect for yourself today?

I Affirm: Today, I will respect myself as the unique and worthy human being that I am.

MARCH **21** *"If you are lonely when you are alone,
you are in bad company."*

— Jean-Paul Sartre

Meditation: Loneliness is purely the ego's way of disrespecting the worthiness of your being and your intimate relationship with the entire Universe. It is merely an illusion and feeling that the ego creates to disconnect you from the oneness of humanity. If you are tuned into your higher self and joined with the positive energy of the Universe you will never be alone. You will always have the collective companionship of the spirit. This is the gift of oneness and the totality of connection with all things.

Ask Yourself: How will you join in and embrace the friendship of the collective spirit of the Universe today?

I Affirm: Today, I will unite with the universal source and bask in the illumination of the spirit.

MARCH **22** *"Act nothing in a furious passion.
It's putting to sea in a storm."*

— Thomas Fuller

Meditation: When anger takes over your mind, you tend to conceal all logic and rationality. The anger burns throughout you and has one purpose and that is to destroy you. In this state, it becomes an extremely dangerous and vulnerable time to engage in any deep thought or decision making concerning your life. In order to be in tune with your inner self and stay on your path to success, it is necessary to allow the anger to come and then allow the anger to drift away. Calm yourself and enter a peaceful state prior to engaging in action or even deep thought. Anger will distort your view of yourself, others, and the world around you.

Ask Yourself: How will you deal with anger in an effective manner and allow action to be taken in a calm and peaceful state of mind?

I Affirm: Today, I will allow anger and frustration to flow through my being without attaching to it for any significant period of time.

MARCH 23 *"Each of us is two selves and the great challenge of life is to try to keep that higher self in command."*

— Dr. Martin Luther King, Jr.

Meditation: Continuously throughout our lives, we struggle with the two opposite sides of our being. As human beings, we sometimes win this fight and sometimes lose this fight. One of the keys of a successful life is being able to choose to live according to your higher self. Always embrace and honor your total being, but when it comes to choosing your behavior do what feels right within. Do not allow your ego to take control; instead, allow your spirit to gently guide you. This guidance will guarantee your search for truth.

Ask Yourself: How will you begin this day with your higher self in command and continue to choose the next right step along your daily journey?

I Affirm: Today, I will rely on the gentle and compassionate guidance of my spirit rather than giving command to my demanding ego.

MARCH 24 *"No one can make you feel inferior without your consent."*

— Eleanor Roosevelt

Meditation: Always remain conscious of the fact that you alone are in complete control of the way in which you react to all people, places, and situations in your life. Your reactions are created within you and are always choices that you make. Do not allow yourself to be controlled by life, but charter your own course. Give yourself the opportunity to feel, think, and behave the way you choose and desire to and a successful life will be within your grasp.

Ask Yourself: How will you take personal responsibility for your reactions and feelings today?

I Affirm: Today, I will regain control of my life and discontinue placing any blame on external people, places, or situations.

March

MARCH 25 *"There is only one problem with saving your dream for someday. Someday will always remain in the future."*
— **Anonymous**

Meditation: Whatever your dreams may be, start to realize them now. Give yourself what you deserve today. If you dream to go to a tropical island, plan the trip. If you want to write a book, start writing. This life belongs to you and it is intended to be a magnificent adventure. Open your mind and eliminate the walls that prevent you from experiencing your dreams and soul felt desires. Begin taking action to live the life you were destined to live. Visualize the results and goals, feel success within you, and truly recognize that you can have anything you want as long as you have the passion and determination to discover your tremendous abilities and power in life.

Ask Yourself: How will you allow yourself to enjoy the gifts of life today and take action to create the life you desire?

I Affirm: Today, I will initiate the beginning of my innovative and creative life.

<hr>

MARCH 26 *"Genius is one percent inspiration and ninety-nine percent perspiration."*
— **Thomas Edison**

Meditation: The reality of life is that we are all exceptional geniuses that were created to complete a small piece of the universal puzzle. Your destiny is to discover this genius and contribute what you were born to do. You are an essential piece of the perfection of the Universe and have the responsibility to give to humanity. There is a secret inside of you that you must uncover. Discover this genius and never give up on this purpose. The Universe and humanity is counting on you and awaits the addition of your specialized brilliance.

Ask Yourself: What is your destined genius? How will you begin to discover and apply this special quality today?

I Affirm: Today, I will unearth my inner brilliance and persist in the direction of my destined purpose.

MARCH 27 *"From error to error, one discovers the entire truth."*

— **Sigmund Freud**

Meditation: Celebrated souls throughout the history of humankind have erred countless times; this will continue to occur infinitely. Without error, the Universe never gets to divulge the entire picture. Error is not failure or the end of a journey, it is merely a sign that guides us on our path to succeeding and lets us know we are getting closer to our desired goal. Error is not meant stop you or slow you down; its function is to motivate you to continue because you are closer now than ever before. From every error something is learned and growth silently takes place in the evolution of your soul and the universal spirit.

Ask Yourself: How will you learn all that you can from your errors today and continue on your excursion to success?

I Affirm: Today, I will welcome errors as essential learning experiences that will aid in my personal and spiritual enhancement.

MARCH 28 *"You can get everything in life you want if you will just help enough other people get what they want."*
— **Zig Ziglar**

Meditation: There is one fact in life that many human beings never realize or tap into the power and potential that it contains. When we help other human beings, we are fulfiling our ultimate purpose and reason for being here on earth. We always feel better when we help another human being and we always increase our self-respect and recognize our worth as a spiritual being; the result of altruistic behavior ultimately leads to the manifestation of contentment and satisfaction in our lives. By aligning with this miraculous power of one human being helping another, we end up on further along our own path to success. Do not allow the chaos of society to smother your genuine necessity to help other human beings. Access and apply this true power and enjoy the fruits of this innate internal purpose we are given as human beings.

Ask Yourself: How will you access your genuine passion to help other human beings today?

I Affirm: Today, I will focus on helping other human beings for the authentic purpose of helping humanity rather than expecting anything in return.

MARCH **29** *"You never achieve success
unless you love what you are doing."*
— Dale Carnegie

Meditation: Living and working with passion, diligence, persistence, and purpose are the main ingredients for success. We cannot possess and apply these attitudes if we do not love what we are doing or why we are living. Do not allow society and your ego to tell you that you must continue to do what you dislike, that you can't do what you desire, or that you are not worthy to live for the purpose you believe in. Search within yourself and determine what you love, what you possess passion for, and why you are here on earth at this very moment. Search for your purpose and then plan to achieve it one step at a time.

Ask Yourself: Are you doing what you love to do? Why not? What will you do today that you truly love? How will you begin to pursue your genuine inner purpose in life? What will be your first step?

I Affirm: Today, I will remind myself that it is never too late to explore and discover my inner most desires; Right now I will begin to walk on the divine path that leads me to this buried treasure.

MARCH **30** *"You must be the change you wish to see in the world."*
— M. K. Gandhi

Meditation: Many people relax and sit down to watch the nightly news and criticize the state of the world . The problem is that these people keep sitting. The solution is not to sit, but to stand up and act. Take control of your life and your purpose and begin to live it passionately. There is within you a piece of the puzzle that will act as a catalyst to transform the world. Don't just sit back and wander along with society, get up and do something, believe, demonstrate, and show the world the momentous change that one human being can create.

Ask Yourself: What will you do to begin living your higher purpose today?

I Affirm: Today, I will not talk about what is needed in the world, but I will live it.

MARCH **31**   *"Put your heart, mind, intellect, and soul into even your smallest acts. This is the secret of success."*
— **Swani Sivananda**

Meditation: There exists no rational or logical excuse not to put your greatest energy into everything you do in your life. To descend to the level of society and the ego and not to exert maximum effort on your journey will yield nothing but mediocrity and tedium in your life. Your soul yearns for you to become the being you were born to be and to break out of the bondage of the ego. To give all that you have got from your mind, body, and soul in all that you experience along your path will bring the much deserved success, as well as the evolution of your spiritual being.

Ask Yourself: How will you begin to discover and apply your inner excellence to everything you do today?

I Affirm: Today, I will demonstrate to the world that I have an unlimited supply of brilliance within my being.

April

APRIL 1 *"Do not go where the path may lead, go instead where there is no path and leave a trail."*

— Anonymous

Meditation: The brilliance and magnificent beauty that the Universe contains is due only to the fact that human beings recognized their spiritual power and abilities and forged ahead creating their own paths that were never stepped on before. They, fortunately, did not follow the trail of mediocrity and weakness that the ego creates, but acted on what was thought to be impossible. If you ignite the fire that burns within you, you will access and align with the power of the Universe. This will allow you to begin your own path and add to the innovation of the world.

Ask Yourself: What path are you going to begin traveling on today, the one that others have trampled on or are you going to create the destined path that burns within you?

I Affirm: Today, I will travel along the spiritual path which is embedded in my soul.

APRIL 2 *"He who lives with the most toys is nonetheless still dead."*

— Author Unknown

Meditation: Throughout our lives, we collect money, property, "things," "stuff," and place enormous value on our collections. We worry about losing them and most of all contemplate how to get more. If you truly assess the worth of these things, you will be surprised. Try collecting other things like memories of those important to you, friendships, love, and gifts you can give humanity. There may be a better investment for you to choose.

Ask Yourself: What will you strive for today?

I Affirm: Today, I will be completely honest with my inner most self and decide what is truly important and precious in my life.

APRIL **3**   *"The best way to predict the future is to invent it."*

— Alan Kay

Meditation: You alone are the architect of your life. You have two choices: One is to follow the lead of the external world and do what society tells you to do or the second option is to follow your genuine self and invent the person you aspire to be. Your heart and soul knows what direction to move and will guide you to the life you were meant to live. If you accept this guidance, the life of your dreams will materialize right in front of your eyes.

Ask Yourself: How will you begin inventing your life according to the guidance of your higher self today?

I Affirm: Today, I will enjoy the creative freedom of being the artist of my own existence.

APRIL **4**   *"In three words I can sum up everything I've learned about life…it goes on."*

— Robert Frost

Meditation: This brief aphorism is simple, yet profound and especially useful as an effective coping skill in life. The fact is that no matter what happens, life will go on and the difficulties will make you stronger. Amazingly, life even goes on after it allegedly ends. We are infinite beings that inhabit this physical world to live, learn, grow, and enhance the development of the Universe. There is no hurry and nothing will put an end to your eternal being. Embrace your infinite self, honor all experiences in your life, and never give up on your personal dreams and desires.

Ask Yourself: How will you embrace your eternal soul today and enjoy life and all the sacred experiences it contains?

I Affirm: Today, I will completely accept the ever-changing Universe and remind myself that "life goes on" as an infinite learning experience.

APRIL **5**   *"Abundance is not something we acquire.*
It's something we tune into."
— **Wayne Dyer**

Meditation: At any moment in our life, we have an enormous amount of wealth encircling us. The question is whether we choose to be grateful for what we have or we deny its existence and descend into self-pity. Ask the Universe for abundance; if you open your eyes and heart you will be fulfiled. The Universe's aspiration is for you to be satisfied and reach your peak potential along your journey. Therefore, it is your job to be open to this energy and allow abundance to transpire in your life.

Ask Yourself: How will you open yourself to abundance today?

I Affirm: Today, I will bathe in the ocean of abundance that has been provided to me by the generous Universe.

APRIL **6**   *"Failure will never overtake me if my determination to*
succeed is strong enough."
— **Og Mandino**

Meditation: Failure is a personal choice that individuals make to discontinue their journey toward success. We often label errors, mistakes, or difficulties with the word failure; however, these are actually stepping-stones along your path to success. Without challenges, there is no personal growth and then success would be meaningless. A true failure is just giving up too soon and not persisting toward the goal in mind. Therefore, failure will never occur as long as you are determined and you persevere until achievement emerges.

Ask Yourself: How can you begin to reframe your thoughts and beliefs about failure today?

I Affirm: Today, I will eliminate failure from my vocabulary and see all challenges and difficulties as crucial growing experiences.

APRIL 7   *"If opportunity doesn't' knock, build a door."*

— Milton Berle

Meditation: Take charge, grab a hold of your life, and create the reality that your higher-self desires and knows is possible. Do not sit passively and wait for the world to hand you anything. Your miraculous existence awaits you; it begins with dreams, desires, beliefs, then actions to seize from life what belongs to you. Within you lives a great purpose and a magnificent imprint of success; it is up to you to allow it to be born and develop in your life.

Ask Yourself: How will you take action and begin creating the success you deserve today?

I Affirm: Today, I will begin working toward the greatness that I know I can achieve in my life.

APRIL 8   *"Opportunities are never lost;*
someone will take the one you miss."

— Unknown Author

Meditation: Keep your eyes open for opportunities for growth on a daily basis. Opportunities are often disguised in challenges, struggles, or difficulties in our life. They are often buried in dirt, covered in dust, or hidden in crevices. Nevertheless, rest assured they are there and, if followed, lead to a profound treasure. Do not miss opportunities in your life by focusing on negative thoughts or emotions. Take advantage of what is being given to you and use it to manifest success and personal growth in your daily life.

Ask Yourself: How will you look for opportunities each moment of your day?

I Affirm: Today, I will practice mindfulness and open myself up to the opportunities that are presented to me throughout the day.

APRIL **9** *"To do nothing is sometimes a good remedy."*

— **Hippocrates**

Meditation: Give yourself a breather today. Sit and relax for a while. Ponder your accomplishments in life and give your mind, body, and soul a break. Life is taxing on a daily basis, therefore it is vital to rest and revive and just allow yourself to be. Giving yourself this precious and essential rest will allow you to become more efficient in your daily life and will allow the silent energy of the Universe to whisper to you. Relax, quiet your mind, and refresh your soul so you can enjoy and take advantage of the opportunities for advancement in all your experiences.

Ask Yourself: When and where will you rest today and give yourself a much deserved break?

I Affirm: Today, I will allow myself a respite from the noise and chaos of society. I will remind myself that I deserve every minute of it.

APRIL **10** *"You see things and say "why?" I dream things that never were and say "why not?"*

— **George Bernard Shaw**

Meditation: Never question your unlimited power to create what you desire in life. Do not ask your ego if you can do something because it has limits, instead, ask your soul, your spirit, your higher self and it will let you know the astonishing power you have to manifest anything you believe you can. Believe, and nothing will impede on your journey. There is nothing different about you or that separates you from the great minds of the past or present. Great achievers believed they could succeed, worked persistently and passionately, and did not give up until they met their goals. This is the secret of remarkable success.

Ask Yourself: How will you tap into your infinite power today and begin your journey to your enormous treasure?

I Affirm: Today, I will join the Universe in pursuit of my ultimate purpose.

APRIL 11 *"Learn all you can from the mistakes of others. You won't have time to make them all yourself."*
— Alfred Sheinwold

Meditation: Historic errors and mistakes made by people around us are the greatest learning experiences present in life. It's a blessing to not have to make our own mistakes to grow, but to use others mistakes as a model of what not to do in life. You do not have to make the devastating and destructive errors of the past to learn; to be a success you must utilize the wisdom and mistakes of others in order to improve your life and the future course of humanity.

Ask Yourself: How will you use historic mistakes and other human being's errors today to expedite your success and minimize your suffering?

I Affirm: Today, I will utilize the valuable lessons of humanity to improve my life.

APRIL 12 *"History will be kind to me for I intend to write it."*
— Winston Churchill

Meditation: Success in life consists of aligning with the burning purpose that exists inside you, then taking control and making it happen. With the ingredients of persistence, courage and confidence, you will successfully manifest this purpose in the world and help humanity to evolve. This is difficult work; however, it is what you are here for. It has been done, continues to be done, and is in your power to make your desires and dreams a part of the universal creation.

Ask Yourself: How will you begin being the sole author of your life's journey today?

I Affirm: Today, I will believe in my ability to achieve my dreams and desires.

April *(handwritten)*

APRIL **13**   *"I cannot teach anybody anything.*
I can only make them think."
— **Socrates**

Meditation: We are continuously learning new philosophies, new ways of living, and various strategies to prosper in life. The possibilities of learning are endless. Nevertheless, learning is vital, but it is not sufficient by itself. Knowledge without integration of thoughts, feelings, and application will not be of any use in your journey toward growth and success. We must integrate what we learn, ponder it, engrave it into our soul, and take action with the passion that lives within our heart. This will be enough for miraculous results.

Ask Yourself: How will you apply the wisdom of the Universe to your life today with passion and determination?

I Affirm: Today, I will seek knowledge from the powerful source of the Universe and apply it in my daily life.

APRIL **14**   *"Knock the 'T' off the CAN'T."*
— **Samuel Johnson**

Meditation: Eliminating one tiny letter from one simple word contained in your vocabulary can transform your life and release the hidden potential within you. Taking this simple step will open your life to limitless and inconceivable experiences. The ultimate universal truth is that human beings have the innate ability and resources to do whatever is desired by taking action with determination, perseverance, and passion. Transform your life today and get CAN'T out of your vocabulary for good.

Ask Yourself: What will you do today that you once told yourself you "CAN'T" do?

I Affirm: Today, I will make a conscious effort to eliminate "CAN'T" from my vocabulary as well as my personal philosophy of living.

APRIL 15   *"There is only one thing more painful than learning from experience, and that is not learning from experience."*

— **Lawrence Peter**

Meditation: Pain, difficulties, adversity, challenges, and all the other expressions associated with this principle are vital aspects of life that transform a human being into a strong, spiritual, and worthwhile man or woman. However, we do not have to face the same difficult experiences repeatedly to learn and grow. Doing this will give you unnecessary pain and suffering. Use difficult experiences to learn and evolve and then move on to the next opportunity for growth. Do not get stuck in the same cycle of misery over and over again. When we do this, we create difficulties for ourselves that are not part of the growth process; they are part of regression rather than progression.

Ask Yourself: What can you learn today from a difficult experience in your life in order to avoid additional and unnecessary pain and suffering?

I Affirm: Today, I will escape the continuous cycle of pain and suffering by learning from my mistakes and not making them over and over again.

⊷⧖⧗⊷

APRIL 16   *"When I listen to my mistakes; I have grown."*

— **Hugh Prather**

Meditation: Without mistakes and errors in life, we do not have the opportunity to grow and awaken our higher selves. To evolve into the being you were designed to be, it is necessary to err, however, it is not necessary to make the same mistake countless times. This adds unnecessary difficulties to life and takes you off your path to spiritual growth. Signs are posted from the Universe and to achieve excellence you must begin to learn from your own experiences rather than constantly repeating the same mistakes. Remember, this is your choice and you may take more time to learn or learn more efficiently.

Ask Yourself: How will you quickly ascertain the life lesson you are meant to learn and move on in your evolutionary process today?

I Affirm: Today, I will reflect on the mistakes that I seem to make countless times and implement a plan to effectively address this area of my life.

APRIL **17** *"The world is your school."*

— **Martin H. Fischer**

Meditation: Everything around us is part of our curriculum and those around us are our fellow students and teachers. Remember to pay attention, listen, and take notes on each and every lesson taught. Of course, you will earn the grade you wish, not in letter form, but in feeling and internal growth. If you are not happy with your grade, you can take any lesson over that you desire. There is no graduation, but there is progress and enlightenment upon your journey. Live, learn, study, experiment, and enjoy your life-long educational voyage.

Ask Yourself: Will you excel in the classroom of life today? How?

I Affirm: Today, I will not judge anything in my life; I will merely treat each moment and each situation as a significant educational experience.

APRIL **18** *"It is the mind that maketh good or ill, that maketh wretch or happy, rich or poor."*

— **Edmund Spenser**

Meditation: Reality and the entirety of our life resides within us, not in the external world. We change and grow by transforming ourselves, thus we have the freedom to thrive, feel, and act according to our internal desire and to create the life we yearn to live. You may choose to live life internally and invent your own experience or live according to the external world and suffer. Change your thoughts, beliefs, and feelings, and you will suddenly notice the evolution of the world around you.

Ask Yourself: How will you create the life you desire today?

I Affirm: Today, I will not fall into the deceitful trap of believing that outside events shape my life.

APRIL **19**   *"Your own mind is a sacred enclosure into which nothing harmful can enter except by your permission."*
— Arnold Bennett

Meditation: Negative and destructive energies often pound at the barriers of your mind and soul for entrance; however, you have the alternative to grant these entrance or decline it. The choice that you make as an individual will be the deciding factor whether you create the life you desire or allow the world and society to control your life's journey. When these negative energies knock, it is helpful to let them know that you are not willing to continue the relationship with them and urge them to move along. This is your personal power; you are destined to succeed if you can follow the signs that are presented to you by the creative and productive universal force.

Ask Yourself: How will you immerse yourself in the positive flow of the Universe rather than allowing the negative influence to triumph over you?

I Affirm: Today, I will allow the ecstasy of the Universe to guide me rather than following the restrictive illusions of society.

APRIL **20**   *"One of the most tragic things I know about human nature is that all of us tend to put off living."*
— Dale Carnegie

Meditation: Life is a playground of endless opportunities for growth, peace, and genuine satisfaction. There are so many precious moments to experience, opportunities for growth, and dreams to be materialized. The Universe wants nothing less than for you to bathe in the experience and bliss of life's journey. Do not deny the opportunity to play and enjoy the pleasures of a truly fulfiled experience that is available for you throughout each moment of everyday. Go play, enjoy, and dance in the rapture of living.

Ask Yourself: What will you do to ensure that you will not postpone living today?

I Affirm: Today, I will become an innocent and blissful child and participate in the blissful harmony of the universal symphony.

APRIL 21   *"What we see depends mainly on what we look for."*

— **Sir John Lubbock**

Meditation: Seek and discover the miraculous in the Universe; it is not difficult to uncover if you submerge your heart and soul in this very moment. Life offers a variety of stimuli and surroundings; we can choose to look at everything in a negative and pessimistic light or choose to see the miracle in everything life has to offer. Open your spirit to the extraordinary and it will manifest in your life. This is already within you, although you must permit it to be born.

Ask Yourself: Are you going to look for all the negativity in life today or will you seek the miraculous the Universe has to offer?

I Affirm: Today, I will make an increased effort to see the sacred and divine in everybody and everything around me.

APRIL 22   *"Going to Church doesn't make you a Christian any more than going to a garage makes you a car."*

— **Lawrence Peter**

Meditation: Anywhere in this Universe, you can experience the divine presence of the creative source. The world is the ultimate cathedral. You can worship your personal creative power in any setting and feel this power within yourself and all beings. We are connected by one creative energy that has one goal, which is the peace and happiness of all creation. If you connect to this force and involve it in everything you do, there is only one destination and that is tranquility and genuine success.

Ask Yourself: How will you connect to the creative force and align with its omnipotent power today?

I Affirm: Today, I will experience the oneness of creation and feel the intensity of this pure consciousness.

APRIL **23**   *"Do the thing you are afraid to do and the death of fear is certain."*

— **Ralph Waldo Emerson**

Meditation: Fear conquers countless individuals and chains them to an existence of monotony and boredom. Without taking risks and allowing faith and hope to enter our lives, we will not reach the potential of our higher self. If you have a desire to accomplish something you must take action and move through it and the fear will promptly diminish. It is actually quite simple to overcome fear; by doing what you fear, it will die with your action.

Ask Yourself: What do you fear and how are you going to begin your journey of conquering this fear today?

I Affirm: Today, I will summon the courage within me and triumph over my restrictive fear.

⋆⟶◯⟵⋆

APRIL **24**   *"Blessed is that man who has found his work."*

— **Elbert Hubbard**

Meditation: Within us is a predestined purpose and passion we are meant to create and fulfill in our lives. This purpose will give you a sense of resolve and meaning in your daily life. To do and be what you were created for is your ultimate passage to the growth and evolution of your soul. Seek, find, and discover what your life is about and enjoy the gifts and blessings that come with living and achieving your ultimate purpose.

Ask Yourself: How can you begin doing what you are truly meant to do today?

I Affirm: Today, I will take just one step toward achieving my supreme purpose; I will remind myself that it is never too late to live according to the passion that burns within my soul.

APRIL 25 *"Forget goals…value the process."*

— Jim Bolton

Meditation: Obviously, we require goals in our lives, however, once we reach a goal we frequently look for the next one to achieve. Far more learning and purpose is in the journey toward our major accomplishments. My goal was a college degree, but the journey was where I received the knowledge and the many opportunities for growth. What happens along the journey is often worth much more in regards to our growth than the specific goal that we are setting out to achieve. Value the illuminating process of life and set out to be the finest human being you can on a daily basis. The achievement of goals will come.

Ask Yourself: How do you plan to enjoy each step your journey today?

I Affirm: Today, I will practice enjoying one moment at a time rather than projecting myself into the future.

APRIL 26 *"It is a mistake to look too far ahead. Only one link in the chain of destiny can be handled at a time."*

— Winston Churchill

Meditation: There exist human beings who have not dealt with the past and continue to experience regret and guilt, and obsess about the impossible action of altering the past the way they desire it to be now. There are also human beings who worry incessantly about the future and its uncertainty. If you continue to live or rather exist this way it is certain that you will not align with your higher purpose because this purpose solely lives in the present moment. Begin to work on the present link in your "chain of destiny" and discard the past and the worries of the future; your life is right now.

Ask Yourself: How can you submerge yourself into the sea of now?

I Affirm: Today, I will make a conscious effort to live my life devoid of the illusions of the past and the future; I will remind myself that life only exists in the present.

APRIL 27

"If we are facing in the right direction, all we have to do is keep on walking."

— Buddhist Saying

Meditation: Reaching success in life is often as simple as continuing on your path and choosing to do the next right thing. If you are aligned with the miraculous power of the universal energy, you will be internally guided to heart and soul felt spiritual success. Get on your chosen path and listen to the guidance of the universal director and you will be well on your way to accomplishing your higher intention. Keep traveling on the illuminated path that has been revealed to you.

Ask Yourself: How will you get on your destined path and continue to travel forward today?

I Affirm: Today, I will assess where my path in life is heading and decide if that's where I truly desire to go.

APRIL 28

"I came to realize that a life lived to help others is the only one that matters and that is my duty... This is my highest and best use as a human."

— Ben Stein

Meditation: If we are not here for the obvious purpose of joining in with the human race and being helpful, what are we on earth for? All the material goods, money, cars, houses, and the rest of our obsessions are useful, I guess, but the only things that truly matter are the hope, inspiration, and the helping hand that we give to other human beings. We are all in the same boat here in the Universe and we might as well join in and row with the others in order to advance in our voyage of life.

Ask Yourself: How can you genuinely help another human being today?

I Affirm: Today, I will venture outside of myself and contribute my love and compassion to humanity.

APRIL **29**

Three Rules of Work:
1. *Out of clutter, find simplicity.*
2. *From discord, find harmony.*
3. *In the middle of difficulty lies opportunity.*

— Albert Einstein

Meditation: Is your life full of clutter, discord, and confusion? Apply these three simple rules proposed by their ingenious author to your professional and personal lives and reap the internal and external rewards to come. Your confusion and chaos will begin to fade away and your struggle with daily living will manifest into opportunities for success. Society often teaches us that complexity, confusion, and chaos are the ways of life; discard this illusion and you are on the path to peace.

Ask Yourself: Develop and implement a plan today in order to utilize these simple but brilliant rules in your daily life. You may be surprised by the benefits you receive! (After all, it probably will not hurt to take a suggestion from Einstein.)

I Affirm: Today, I will live my life with simplicity and ease; I will not over-complicate and intellectualize everything in my path.

APRIL **30**

"Success is 95% failure."

— Soichiro Honda

Meditation: You may not realize the enormous amount of success you have achieved in your lifetime. Human beings tend to allow society to define success; however, what does society perceive success as? The man who hits home runs or the individual who offers food to a homeless person? The lawyer who defends the guilty criminal or the counselor who passionately helps suffering human being? Sports professionals are paid millions of dollars, how much do front line helping professionals make make? Which headline is likely to be on a newspaper? "Giants Win the Super Bowl" or "Unknown Man Helps Handicapped Man Cross the Street"?

Ask Yourself: How can you allow your spirit to be successful today and ignore society's definition of success?

I Affirm: Today, I will independently and personally define genuine success in my life.

MAY 1 *"In the faces of men and women I see God."*

— **Walt Whitman**

Meditation: The creative energy we call God is the essence of everything and every being that surrounds us. There is one distinct force in the Universe that unites us. If we connect and align with this force, we will be filled with positive energy that provides for prosperity and authentic success. You will give birth to the potential and possibilities that inhabit your being. Feel this, live this, and allow it to radiate from your heart and soul.

Ask Yourself: How will you recognize and embrace the sacred in everything around you today?

I Affirm: Today, I will open my eyes to the miracle of existence and admire beauty of my surroundings.

MAY 2 *"Whosoever asks you to go with him one mile, go two."*

— **Jesus**-from Sermon on the Mount

Meditation: Aspire to be the most determined and passionate person in everything you do. No matter what you do along your journey of life, do it your very best and persevere until you succeed. Constantly do more than what is expected of you and you will be astounded by the results of your extra effort. This will bring you success and increase your worth and esteem as a special being of the Universe.

Ask Yourself: In what part of your life will you begin to go above and beyond today? Transfer this to all other aspects of your life and watch success accumulate consistently.

I Affirm: Today, I will travel the extra mile in everything I do without expecting anything in return.

MAY 3   *"If you can find a path with no obstacles it probably doesn't lead anywhere."*

— Frank A. Clark

Meditation: Embrace every challenge that is set before you. These challenges will mold you into the individual you are destined to be. They will create spirituality within you; they will build courage and test your limits. They will demonstrate and clarify the importance of persistence in all your endeavors. They will eventually transform you into a human being with meaning and purpose that does not allow adversity to interrupt their travels.

Ask Yourself: How will you begin to perceive challenges and difficulties today as the bedrock of who you become and what you accomplish on your journey?

I Affirm: Today, I will face all my trials and tribulations with courage, excitement, and determination; I will remind myself that how I handle these adversities define my character.

MAY 4   *"It's time to start living the life you imagined."*

— Henry James

Meditation: Human beings often take advantage of and ignore the precious nature of life and the possibilities it contains. If you are just merely getting by or existing in a monotonous life, please reflect and contemplate the special opportunity you have and the limitless possibilities that are right in front of you. Whatever you can imagine or dream, you can create in your life. Believe and take action and you will experience amazing results. Wash away the debris of the ego and the deception of society and tap into the truth and innocence that you once enjoyed. Go and challenge life for what you believe and what you desire.

Ask Yourself: How will you begin to materialize the dreams and desires that you once had as a young idealistic traveler on life's journey?

I Affirm: Today, I will believe in myself as an individual that is capable of achieving anything I put my heart and soul into.

MAY **5**

"There are only two ways to live your life. One as though nothing is a miracle, the other as though everything is a miracle."

— **Albert Einstein**

Meditation: If you take an in depth and reflective look at the Universe, you will see and understand the miraculous in life. Just look at the sky, the variety of species, the sea, the flowers, and all of the other aspects of perfection in this world. Think of the miracle of birth, one cell developing into the perfection of a human being. If you ponder and contemplate the precision and the flawlessness of life, you have no other choice then to see the miraculous. The choice is yours; live miraculously or live monotonously.

Ask Yourself: Will you think of the miraculous today or plummet into the trap of negativity?

I Affirm: Today, or actually right this moment, I will observe and reflect on the various miracles that surround me.

MAY **6**

"Nothing diminishes anxiety faster than action."

— **Walter Anderson**

Meditation: We live in an age of anxiety. In our lives, we are taught and expected to be anxious, overwhelmed and frustrated. If we do not exhibit these characteristics; we are thought to be lazy, unsuccessful, or abnormal in some strange sense. There are many problems with this expectation, one being that anxiety is dangerous to our health as well as incredibly unproductive in our daily life. Therefore, society's viewpoint is destructive and we need to live healthy rather than up to the expectations of the world around us. Seek peace and live in the moment and you will experience a substantial difference in your life.

Ask Yourself: How will you seek serenity today rather than anxiety?

I Affirm: Today, I will absorb the tranquility and serenity that is available in the present moment rather than adopt the chaos and anxiety of the world around me.

MAY 7   *"The question is not whether we will die, but how we will live."*

— **Joan Borynsenko**

Meditation: Death is inevitable; however, life is a choice that we make on a daily basis. We can choose to live today or merely exist and waste precious time. You will eventually die and move on, but will you merely exist in life or will you live genuinely and courageously? This is truly up to you and only you. Tap into your inner resources and create the life you once dreamed of as a child. It is your time to shine in the illumination of life.

Ask Yourself: Will you live with sincerity today?

I Affirm: Today, I will choose to live my life with courage and passion.

MAY 8   *"To know even one life has breathed easier because you lived—this is to have succeeded."*

— **Ralph Waldo Emerson**

Meditation: To help another human being throughout our journey of life is a precious gift and an absolute miracle. This ability is priceless and actually adds meaning and purpose to one's life. There will never be a time when helping another human being does not add worth and excellence to your life as a member of the human race. Lending your hand to another human being is the quintessence of life. Fulfill this purpose and you have lived. Give from the passion of your heart and you have succeeded.

Ask Yourself: Who will you lend your hand to today?

I Affirm: Today, I will emanate unconditional love and compassion from my inner most being.

May

MAY **9**

"It is not death that a man should fear, but he should fear never beginning life."

— **Marcus Aurelius**

Meditation: Fear of death often plagues our minds and our souls. This takes energy that can more efficiently be used for living. Begin to embrace and see death as a celebration to another dimension of living. Once death is accepted as an inevitable part of life, moving on with actual living can take place. We are infinite beings that exist in different dimensions of life. There is no end; it is all merely a journey. The acceptance of death and not knowing when it will occur can actually improve your ability to value and appreciate the things in your life that truly matter.

Ask Yourself: How will you accept death and consciously live today? If you were on your deathbed right now at this moment, what would you regret not doing and not paying attention to?

I Affirm: Today, I will focus my attention on the things I may regret if I were to depart this earth today and I will be certain to begin being mindful of these valuable elements of my life on a daily basis.

MAY **10**

"We are self made victims of mediocrity."

— **Norman Vincent Peale**

Meditation: Do not allow yourself to fall prey to the negativity of your ego. Your spirit does not desire average living or mediocrity from you, but desires nothing less than brilliance and exceptional performance. Life is too precious to allow it to waste away without pursuing your fantasies and heart felt desires. Journey to the depths of your being and discover your uniqueness, your excellence, and your impeccable ability to invent a life of success and unlimited happiness. Believe in this reality and begin creating it right now.

Ask Yourself: How will you access your spirit today and move beyond the Mediocrity of your ego?

I Affirm: Today, I will transcend my ego and access the powerful divinity that resides within me.

MAY **11** *"Courage does not always roar. Sometimes courage is the small, quiet voice at the end of the day saying, 'I will try again tomorrow'."*

— Author Unknown

Meditation: It is imperative that you are persistently tuned into the quiet, yet powerful voice within you. This voice can often help you tap into the evocative inspiration of your soul and guide you to where the Universe wishes you to be. Often, the battle to overcome challenges and difficulties is silent, yet courageous and determined. Do not be discouraged by stillness and peace in your life, just listen and patiently move through your difficulties with purpose and audacity.

Ask Yourself: How will you allow the silent voice within you to speak and be clearly attended to today?

I Affirm: Today, I will allow the gentle whisper of courage to express itself in my life.

MAY **12** *"Be kind for everyone you meet is fighting a harder battle."*

— Plato

Meditation: As you are already aware of, life consists of countless challenges and difficulties that are actually responsible for creating who we are and actualizing who our higher self desires for us to become. We are also an important part of the human race where others are in the same realization process as we are. There is no better way to progress and move forward on our path then to be kind to ourselves and others who are battling with life on a daily basis. Kindness is the secret ingredient to personal and spiritual enlightenment.

Ask Yourself: What will you do to be kind to yourself today? Additionally, what will you do to show your kindness to other human beings today?

I Affirm: Today, I will recognize that others may be struggling just as I am , therefore all my actions will be overflowing with compassion and kindness.

MAY **13**   *"We turn to God for help when our foundations are shaking, only to learn that it is God who is shaking them."*

— Charles West

Meditation: Our creator is our cherished friend, our teacher, our lover, our healer, our reliever, and above all a part of our spirit. This creative spirit has enormous power and the capacity to do anything and everything, therefore we also possess this ability because this identical creative energy resides within our being. This universal energy knows exactly what we need to learn in our journey and often has a part in creating these necessary learning experiences in our life. When life appears to be unstable, confusing, and arduous, keep in mind that it is highly probable that your creator is confronting you with an opportunity for learning and personal development.

Ask Yourself: How will you honor and grow from the trembling of your foundation today?

I Affirm: Today, I will see challenges as exactly what they are, experiences to help me to evolve in my spiritual quest.

MAY **14**   *"All that I am or hope to be, I owe to my angel mother."*

— Abraham Lincoln

Meditation: Mothers are sacred beings with the unique characteristics of angels. They were blessed with the ability to love unconditionally and do their absolute best with the resources that they have. They were sent down from the heavens to fulfill their role of angels on earth. You may mistakenly forget to honor and appreciate the gifts that your mother has given you throughout your life, especially the most important gift of life. Honor your mother today and everyday by being and becoming the person she would want you to be.

Ask Yourself: How has your mother been an angel in your life? Tell your mother or mother figure in your life how you feel and appreciate her; if she has passed write a letter and communicate with her eternal spirit. (She's probably the one guiding you along your journey.)

I Affirm: Today, I will honor my mother or mother figure in my life for the unconditional love and acceptance she has provided me.

MAY **15** *"Wisdom begins with wonder."*

— Socrates

Meditation: A life filled with wonder, curiosity, and amazement will certainly lead to wisdom and spiritual evolution. Travel along your journey seeking adventure and living the life your higher self desires. Do not fall victim to society and the negative influence of those around you, be a creator and resist being created by external forces. Continuously immerse yourself in the miraculous and the mystery of this vast Universe.

Ask Yourself: How will you live life as an adventure today?

I Affirm: Today, I will seek adventure in my life like I once did as an excited and curious child.

MAY **16** *"If you think you can do a thing or think you can't do a thing, you're right."*

— Henry Ford

Meditation: All our efforts as human beings come from our own expectations and beliefs about ourselves. If you continuously doubt yourself, you are certain to prove this in your life. If you believe in yourself, you are certain to accomplish astounding things and even things that you once thought impossible. Take this power of belief and positive thinking and run with it. The power of belief and visualizing results in your life are miraculous, but do not take my word for it, get out there, experiment, and profit from your persistence.

Ask Yourself: What will you believe you can do today that you once thought impossible?

I Affirm: Today, I will utilize the power of visualization and belief in my life to manifest my utmost desires.

MAY 17

"It is impossible for a man to learn what he thinks he already knows."

— Epictetus

Meditation: Keep your mind open and life will present you with the opportunity to learn extraordinary lessons. Open-mindedness is imperative if you desire success and personal growth. Those with open minds are able to break through the barriers of society and create a life for themselves. Regardless of the amount of knowledge we possess or acquire in our lifetime, we will only know a small percentage of the knowledge available in this infinite world. Open yourself to the vast wisdom of the Universe and watch your life transform drastically.

Ask Yourself: How will you keep an open mind today, free of biases and judgments in order to take advantage of the lessons of the Universe?

I Affirm: Today, I will be honest with myself and admit that I really don't know as much as I think I do about life and reality.

MAY 18

"The most beautiful thing we can experience is mysteriousness. It is the source of all true art and science."

— Albert Einstein

Meditation: For comfort and safety, we often desire to know everything about everything or at least think we know everything about everything. We define, categorize, and create tight boxes or containers to keep everything in. Actually, the control that we attempt to create is illusory. The reality of life is that it is mysterious and the sooner we learn to have peace in this fact and move on, the sooner we will begin to enjoy life and all of its freedoms. We do not need to know everything to be peaceful.

Ask Yourself: How will you work on accepting the mystery of life today and strive for peace and wonder within it?

I Affirm: Today, I will not try to label everything in life according to my perceptions; I will simply accept life as life and just be in this very moment.

MAY **19** *"Genius means little more than the faculty of perceiving in an unhabitual way."*

— William James

Meditation: Allow yourself to escape the powerful restraints of ordinary everyday societal thinking and begin to converse with your inner genius. This is your creative and spiritual self that is liberated from societal and habitual modes of thought, feeling, and behavior. Your inner genius is psychologically free from the boundaries of the ordinary and monotonous. It is imperative to realize that what society teaches is not always the truth and what the majority of people believe is not always reality or the most effective way to perceive reality. Follow the guidance of your innate genius and you will not be lead astray.

Ask Yourself: How will you allow your inner genius to have freedom today rather than tying it down?

I Affirm: Today, I will follow the guidance of my spiritual intelligence rather than being directed by the thinking of the majority.

MAY **20** *"Nothing is impossible unless one agrees that it is."*

— Og Mandino

Meditation: The word "impossible" is another example of a destructive, negative, and useless utterance that we continue to allow in our vocabulary. This word is not real; however, it has created great blocks and barriers for human beings since the beginning of time. Things are not impossible; we make things impossible by labeling them so. Discard this word and do not allow it to affect your life from this moment on.

Ask Yourself: What is your strategy to rid yourself of the word "impossible" today and eternally in your life?

I Affirm: Today, I will break through the restraints of self doubt and realize that anything I desire is possible in my life.

MAY 21 *"People living deeply have no fear of death."*

— Anais Nin

Meditation: Fear of anything that will eventually become a reality in life no matter what we do is unproductive and irrational. Fear of death is disabling in our attempt to live the life we were created to live. Faith and hope, on the other hand, enables us to walk through fear and reach for success. Action combined with faith and hope is the secret to ridding yourself of fear. Become action-oriented in your pursuit toward success and fear becomes unnecessary.

Ask Yourself: How will you begin to take the necessary action in order to rid yourself of fear today?

I Affirm: Today, I will not attach to irrational fear , but I will walk through it with courage and resolve.

MAY 22 *"Success is the ability to go from one failure to another with no loss of enthusiasm."*

— Winston Churchill

Meditation: Enthusiasm sets us apart from those caught up in the chaotic rat race of the ego. Be enthusiastic about your life continuously and you will quickly catch up to success and bypass all the rubbish of your ego. Failure as seen by the ego is a very negative event in our life, however, when we look at failure in the eyes of our spirit we see the truth; failure brings us closer to our goal and teaches us endurance and perseverance along the way. Welcome failure along your path and face it with courage and zest.

Ask Yourself: How will you face life with unending enthusiasm today and embrace failure as a way to grow and evolve?

I Affirm: Today, I will clearly perceive any so-called "failure" in my life as a vital stepping stone on my path toward genuine success and joy.

MAY 23 *"What we think of as 'sacred' actually is present in everything we do."*

— Riane Eisler

Meditation: If you look at life in a detailed and sincere manner, you will recognize how sacred everyone and everything is around you. Everything we see, do, and come into contact with is sacred; however, society has attempted to erase this attribute of the Universe. Take back your ability to recognize and feel everything as sacred and dance in the elegance of life. Each moment of each day is precious and needs to be appreciated for its essence.

Ask Yourself: How will you recognize and appreciate the sacred in everything today?

I Affirm: Today, I will approach each moment as being more precious and sacred than the previous.

MAY 24 *"First keep the peace within yourself, then you can also bring peace to others."*

— Thomas Kempis

Meditation: Peace in life is created by energy sources from the internal to the external. Nothing outside of you will bring you peace; you must first choose it and then create it from within. Then, you will contain the energy of peace to emanate from within you to others. Always remain conscious that peace, success, and personal transformation initiate from within, then, after hard work, can be manifested in your external life. Reaching outside and expecting peace and happiness is the great illusion of the world. Do not be fooled by this.

Ask Yourself: How will you create peace within your inner life today?

I Affirm: Today, I will remember that my external life is created from within.

May

MAY 25 *"Pushing through fear is less frightening than living with the underlying fear that comes from a feeling of helplessness."*
— Susan Jeffers

Meditation: Facing fear head on is what allows us to grow and succeed in life. To do only what is comfortable is giving up on the challenge and adventure of our existence. Take action to move through fear and you will gain self worth, strength, and the power to live the life you desire. To sit back and allow life to live you is not what we are here to succumb to. Take control and risk success in your life rather than living with the underlying feeling of being controlled.

Ask Yourself: What fear will you face head on today and show the Universe that you truly desire success?

I Affirm: Today, I will treat my fear as a valuable instrument in my journey toward personal enlightenment.

-><==)(==-<-

MAY 26 *"Anger makes you smaller while forgiveness forces you to grow beyond what you were."*
— Cherie Carter-Scott

Meditation: Anger involves conflict with the spiritual essence of your being and with the eternal growth process, which results in nothing but suffering and negative energy along your journey. Let go of anger today, replace it with the courage and strength of forgiveness, and experience the illumination this will add to your life .

Ask Yourself: What or who are you angry with today and how will you embark on the necessary process of forgiveness?

I Affirm: Today, I will give myself the priceless gift of forgiveness rather than harboring the weight of anger and resentment.

MAY **27** *"Whatever you are be a good one."*

— Abraham Lincoln

Meditation: Whatever it is that you do for a living or the role you take in life, you are just as important as everyone else around you. You have the ability and blueprint within you to be the best of whatever your individual purpose is in life. Do not fall into the trap that society creates concerning the status of different professions and roles. Do what you love and perform it beyond what is expected of you and you will be successful internally and externally.

Ask Yourself: How will you plan to be phenomenal today in everything you do?

I Affirm: Today, I will present my extraordinary self to the world.

MAY **28** *"Stop clinging to your personality and see all beings as yourself. Such a person could be entrusted with the whole world."*

— Lao Tzu

Meditation: To truly comprehend and honor the union of all human beings is the most astonishing and brilliant realization that one can ever have. The human race and the entire Universe is one; this will eventually be revealed to all of humanity, however, the sooner you realize this, the more progress will be made in life and the world around us. Begin living this vital and transforming revelation today.

Ask Yourself: How will you manifest and honor oneness and unity among all in your life today?

I Affirm: Today, I will live according to the supreme truth of unity; I will feel my connection to all of humanity.

MAY **29**   *"The wisest mind has something yet to learn."*

— **George Santayana**

Meditation: To truly believe that you know the entirety of anything is pure foolishness. We only have knowledge of what our mind believes to be the truth, but we all possess our individualized truths. Always be open and willing to learn other human being's truths and beliefs. Our truths are always changing and evolving and this is the pure beauty of life and our vast range of experiences. Never close your mind to the world; this is the one mistake that you cannot afford to make.

Ask Yourself: How will you open yourself up today to a new reality?

I Affirm: Today, I will be open-minded and willing to learn from others; I will be comfortable saying," I don't know".

MAY **30**   *"The ideal day never comes.*
Today is ideal for him who makes it so."
— **Horatio Dresser**

Meditation: We often hear countless people express that "someday they will be happy," "that day will come," "I'm going to be happy when I find a new job, get a university degree, find a perfect lover." Why not take advantage of this very moment and make this the day you decide to be peaceful, happy, and content? Future happiness is a goal that will not be achieved if present happiness is not a priority. Absolutely nothing external has the power to make you happy; happiness must be a choice decided from within.

Ask Yourself: What is stopping you from choosing and creating true success and genuine happiness in your life or are you comfortable in your self-made hole?

I Affirm: Today, I will break out of my self made comfort zone and choose success.

MAY 31   *"Things that hurt instruct."*

— **Benjamin Franklin**

Meditation: Emotional pain can be an immense challenge in life, although we often learn great lessons through struggles and anguish. We learn significant lessons about our inner self and the things that need to be changed in our lives. Always remember that pain is only temporary and should be used for the purpose of growth and the evolution of your being. When you feel pain today, ask yourself what you can learn and what needs to be changed within you.

Ask Yourself: What was a lesson from the past that was painful but valuable?

I Affirm: Today, I will transform the pain in my life into a tool for internal growth and development.

JUNE **1**   *"Begin with the end in mind."*

— **Stephen Covey**

Meditation: Often, we deny ourselves the power that we truly possess within to create what we desire in life. We are equipped with an unlimited supply of energy and a luminous spirit that has the ability to manifest what we passionately desire. If you know what you want in life the Universe will provide you with everything you need to obtain this dream. One thing you must do is prove to the universal power that you are willing to go to any lengths to achieve this internal aspiration.

Ask Yourself: What do you truly and passionately want in life? Write it down in a safe place and repeat it to yourself on a daily basis. Visualize all aspects of this accomplishment as if it had already happened and it will soon appear in your life.

I Affirm: Today, I will confidently believe in my ability to achieve what I desire in my life. I will achieve.

JUNE **2**   *"Whenever I hear it can't be done,*
I know I'm close to success."

— **Michael Flatley**

Meditation: Allow the "can'ts" that others create for you in your life to energize your soul. Your motivation will increase if you aim to teach those unfortunate individuals that nothing is impossible. It is vital that you never tell yourself that something can't be achieved in your life because this would be an erroneous belief. Anything you passionately pursue can and will be achieved as long as you ask the Universe for assistance and never give up. Passion, persistence, and determination destroy all the "can'ts" that were once a part of your life.

Ask Yourself: How will you protect yourself from the pessimism of society and move forward toward your goals that you know within your soul to be possible?

I Affirm: Today, I will firmly believe that I CAN accomplish anything I truly desire.

JUNE 3

"For those who will fight bravely and not yield, there is a triumphant victory over all the dark things of life."
— **James Allen**

Meditation: There are two important ingredients for the transformation of the world as well as genuine personal success. Never lose hope in anyone or anything and never give up on your unique purpose in this Universe. If you combine these two ingredients in every challenge of your life, you will always prevail. It is only when you give in to the distortions and delusions of the world that you will be defeated.

Ask Yourself: What purpose are you willing to fight for today?

I Affirm: Today, I will unleash the spiritual warrior within me and battle for what I believe in.

JUNE 4

"We hate some persons because we do not know them; and will not know them because we hate them."
— **Charles Caleb Colton**

Meditation: Hatred throughout this world has caused endless suffering and threatens to destroy the quality of living we desire. Hatred only harms those that hate and eats away at the core of your heart and soul. It ruins your experience of life and takes away great opportunities for growth and learning. Get to know the people and things that you dislike and you will know a new way of living. Discard judgments and begin to see all you meet as part of you and teachers on your path to personal and spiritual advancement.

Ask Yourself: How will you gain knowledge of people and areas of life that you are ignorant of? Are you capable of loving all members of the human race?

I Affirm: Today, I will sincerely contemplate my ignorance concerning humanity and begin to live according to the spiritual principle of unity.

JUNE **5**   *"Every burden is a blessing."*

— **Robert Schuller**

Meditation: Life is crammed with overwhelming challenges and difficulties. These trying times are parts of life when we truly grow and enlighten the unborn spirit within us. Take a step back and be grateful for these opportunities to truly evolve into who you are. Every challenge and difficulty you face has a distinct lesson hidden within; it is your responsibility to unearth this message and decode its special memorandum unique to your life's passage.

Ask Yourself: How will you begin to truly embrace and realize the meaning and worthwhile experience available in every challenge presented in your life?

I Affirm: Today, I will be grateful for the adversity in my life because without it I know I would not become the person I wish to be.

JUNE **6**   *"Determination, patience, and courage are the only things needed to improve any situation."*

— **Unknown Author**

Meditation: It is extremely essential in life to recognize and internalize the fact that everything changes and all difficult times will soon pass. You have the power to speed up this process by utilizing your spiritual energy while incorporating these three qualities mentioned above. Any demanding situation in your life can be used for further growth and as an opportunity to learn the essential lessons that your soul has attracted into your life.

Ask Yourself: What situation will you apply these principles to today and how will you incorporate these in your daily life?

I Affirm: Today, I will implement a plan to improve my capacity to utilize these three indispensable elements in my life.

JUNE 7   *"Like what you do. If you don't like it do something else."*

— Paul Harvey

Meditation: Do not deceive yourself by believing that you are "stuck" where you are at right now. You may wish to rationalize or justify this to others; however, it is important to realize that anything is possible with hard work and persistence. Never allow yourself to fall into the delusion of society or the world around you when it tells you that you must stay in one profession for a lifetime. You have the freedom to move on and move up anytime you please. Fulfill your intrinsic needs and take part in the passionate excursion of your life.

Ask Yourself: If you do not like where you are at, what you do, or who you are, take action now. What change will you initiate today?

I Affirm: Today, I will free myself from the limitations of society and allow my genuine self to begin making decisions.

JUNE 8   *"Character consists of what you do on the third and fourth tries."*

— John Albert Michener

Meditation: Succeeding on the first attempt on any task in your life makes you a lucky person, but continuing to persevere and persist on your path following difficulties and defeats makes you a true genius. Each failure is an achievement towards spiritual perfection. All distinguished men and women throughout history have failed numerous times, although never perceived themselves as failures; they simply battled on each day following their failures as signs to success.

Ask Yourself: What will you continue to do despite setbacks you have experienced?

I Affirm: Today, I will continue to move forward regardless of what or who stands in my way.

JUNE 9

"We are here to add what we can to life not to get what we can from it."

— William Osler

Meditation: We often take, take, and take from the Universe and live under the illusion that these material things will complete our lives. Well, if you want the secret of completing your life, begin to give to the Universe rather than seeking what you can have for yourself. The great achievements in life are not what we receive or the awards we obtain, but are the special gifts that we give to humanity. These contributions are the only things we can leave the world with genuine significance and lasting value.

Ask Yourself: What will you give to the Universe today?

I Affirm: Today, I will refuse to give in to my selfish desires.

JUNE 10

"Courage is being afraid but going on anyhow."

— Dan Rather

Meditation: I'm sure that you can identify countless things you are fearful of in life, however, if deep-down you desire to be involved in these things do not allow fear to hold you back. Face it head on and grasp that which you desire. Fear is a universal indication that these things are worth striving for. Face the fear and differentiate yourself from the others that do not pursue what they want and deserve in life. Progressing onward despite fear is the greatest developmental experience you will engage in along your precious journey.

Ask Yourself: What will you do to walk through fear today and pursue your well deserved desires?

I Affirm: Today, I will recognize and honor my fear , however I will not allow it to hold me back from anything in life.

JUNE 11   *"He who has a why to live can bear almost any how."*

— **Nietzsche**

Meditation: Beyond all tasks our life is overflowing with, discovering the purpose that is etched in our soul is most vital. Look within and uncover the treasure of your spirit that has been waiting patiently for unearthing. Discovering and following this intrinsic purpose in your life will enhance your ability to move through obstacles daily and succeed in everything you do. This is the secret to personal enlightenment and maximum success.

Ask Yourself: Can you search deep within yourself today and truly ask your spirit why you are here?

I Affirm: Today, I will remember to listen carefully to the soft , but powerful voice of my spirit

JUNE 12   *"The best way to know God is to love many things."*

— **Vincent van Gogh**

Meditation: Love is the essence of the creative source. Love conquers all within this Universe. To love and be loved is to live according to your universal design. Seek to follow the path of love and you will find the source of this miraculous creation. Love is the key to worldly transformation. If you desire to be united to the collective consciousness of the Universe, it is imperative to passionately be in love with all things and all beings you come into contact with. Peruse your surroundings and express your love for the miraculous in the world.

Ask Yourself: How will you express your intoxicating ability to love today?

I Affirm: Today, I will explore the immense love contained within my heart and allow it radiate from my entire being.

JUNE **13**   *"Failure is the path of least persistence."*

— Unknown Author

Meditation: Failure is a choice we consciously make. There are always alternative routes that can be taken that lead to success. Keep moving forward, keep fighting, keep working, and you are bound to succeed. Perseverance and persistence are always the answer. Connect to the source of all beings and continue to follow this guidance despite the difficulties along your path. Directly through these negative energies is the way to personal and spiritual growth. It is simply the world's way of making you work for your upcoming victories.

Ask Yourself: What will you persist toward today in order to move closer to your ultimate purpose?

I Affirm: Today, I will set out to conquer all obstacles in my path to success.

JUNE **14**   *"The soul never thinks without a mental picture."*

— Aristotle

Meditation: The soul will present you with a visually detailed depiction of its dreams and desires. You must tap into the spirit and quintessence of your being and begin to allow these pictures to guide you in your pursuit of success. These visualizations will reveal the deepest and most desired dreams and paths that your soul has designed for exclusively for you. It is your obligation to connect to the energy within and follow the guidance it offers.

Ask Yourself: Can you describe the pictures of your soul and begin illustrating them in your daily life?

I Affirm: Today, I will align with the creative energy of my soul and begin manifesting my deepest desires.

JUNE **15** *"It's easy to make a buck.*
It's a lot tougher to make a difference."
— Tom Brockaw

Meditation: Obsession with money appears to preside over everyone and everything around us. Of course it's needed, however, to hoard it or center your whole life around making it, saving it, and spending it is a great disgrace to this Universe. If you are not making a difference, what are you here for? Your essential source has a higher plan for you rather than revolving around monetary rewards and material possessions, it is wholly up to you to discover this plan and begin revealing it in your life. If you desire temporary pleasure and an illusory sense of control continue developing your monetary foundation in life, if you choose genuine happiness, peace, and true success begin making a difference in the world today.

Ask Yourself: How will you choose to make a difference today rather then basing your value and worth on dollars and cents?

I Affirm: Today, I will endeavor to make a difference another human being's life.

JUNE **16** *"We all have ability: the difference is how we use it."*

— Stevie Wonder

Meditation: Human beings often look outside of themselves to other individuals and admire or idolize their marvelous abilities rather than looking within and searching for their own remarkable talents. I learned a while ago that I am no different from the people I admire and the people I derive inspiration from. I just need to discover my unique ability and apply it in my life. Rather than looking to the external world for inspiration, look within and begin to utilize the enormous amount of resources contained within you. Realize the great abilities that are living silently inside of you waiting for their chance to experience excellence in your life. Admire and inspire yourself rather than those outside of you.

Ask Yourself: What is your innate genius and how can you begin admiring it today?

I Affirm: Today, I will look within myself for inspiration.

JUNE **17**

"A strong passion…will ensure success.
For the desire of the end will point out the means."
— William Hazlitt

Meditation: When you truly, with all your heart and soul, know exactly what you desire in life, you will be shown exactly how to accomplish this by the power of the Universe. Listen to your inner guide and rid it of the uncertainty and doubt created by society around you. Go and align with the creative energy of the Universe and move toward success. This success will begin to manifest each day in your life as long as you persist with passionate determination and continuously visualize the details of your desires.

Ask Yourself: What do you imagine when you visualize your success? Describe all aspects in your mind and move forward to accomplish this. Be patient and the Universe will show you the path.

I Affirm: Today, I will practice patience and wait for the direct me on the path to success.

JUNE **18**

"We must overcome the notion that we must be regular…it
robs you of the chance to be extraordinary and leads you to
the mediocre."
— Uta Hagan

Meditation: Mediocrity, typical, ordinary, and conformity are all the expressions that society would like you to embrace and internalize in your life. To fit in is to turn your back on your spirit and allow society to define your life. Break out of this mold and become the unique, special, and brilliant human being that you were created to be. Take your personal power back from the external force of society and live according to your higher-self.

Ask Yourself: How will you give your soul life today and break out of the boundaries created by society and your ego?

I Affirm: Today, I will express the unique qualities of my spirit and exude greatness rather than mediocrity.

JUNE **19**   *"It can be said that God cannot be known in the mind but only experienced in the heart."*

— **Stephen Levine**

Meditation: Faith in what is beyond us is stored in the heart and can only be felt, our intellect is controlled by our ego, this we need to move beyond and begin experiencing the Universe without intellectualizing the experience away. Not entirely comprehending the divine source is exactly how it is supposed to be, this allows you to develop hope and faith in the mysteries of the Universe and transform your corporeal being into a spiritually enlightened individual.

Ask Yourself: How will you feel the omnipotent power of the cosmos today?

I Affirm: Today, I will rely on my capacity to feel the sacred in the Universe rather than attempting to figure it out intellectually.

JUNE **20**   *"He that won't be counseled can't be helped."*

— **Benjamin Franklin**

Meditation: Continue to demonstrate open-mindedness and willingness to be guided by those who you trust and those who possess great wisdom. Allow yourself to be teachable in order to learn, internalize, and apply the principles of success. Ask for help and apply this guidance to your life. Human beings were created to depend on each other in order to join as one and succeed in life.

Ask Yourself: Whose help will you ask for today? How will you prepare yourself to be open and amenable to the counsel and wisdom of other human beings around you?

I Affirm: Today, I will be willing to have faith and trust in another human being , instead of doing everything myself.

JUNE 21   *"Whoever I am, or whatever I am doing, some kind of excellence is within my reach."*
— **John W. Gardner**

Meditation: We are brought into this world destined for excellence. Separation between our will and the Universe's destiny prevents us from achieving this success. Get back on your destined path and create the excellence that is imprinted in your soul. Surround yourself with people of success; immerse yourself in thoughts, beliefs, visions, dreams, and feelings of triumph and you will be prepared to achieve greatness.

Ask Yourself: How will you work toward your internally encoded success today?

I Affirm: Today, I will give nothing less than my very best in each individual moment.

JUNE 22   *"Great things are not done by impulse, but by a series of small things brought together."*
— **Vincent van Gogh**

Meditation: If you have the ability to take one small step in the right direction, you are capable of greatness. We often believe acts of greatness are achieved all at one moment in one miraculous act, however, the reality is that small simple miraculous acts add up into one creation of greatness; we all have the ability to take these small steps and add them together to equal extraordinary success. Belief in yourself and the connection to the force around you will give you the ability to bring immense achievements into fruition.

Ask Yourself: What small step toward greatness will you take today? What is it that you wish to accomplish?

I Affirm: Today, I will take the initial step toward something great and make a commitment to persevere until completion of my goal.

JUNE **23**

"Successful people do the things that failures are afraid to tackle."

— Og Mandino

Meditation: There is no such thing as a failure. Failure is a delusion created by the ego and society. Each one of us has success programmed within our being, however, we must choose to access this and follow the path ingrained within us. You are one with success-now choose it as part of your reality starting right now. Do not allow any obstacle, challenge, person, false belief, or dogmatic illusion to prevent you from what the Universe has designed specifically for your life.

Ask Yourself: What will you do today that you once feared and thought to be beyond your reach?

I Affirm: Today, I will follow the program for success that the Universe has provided me.

JUNE **24**

"The unhappiness of mortals is that man who insists upon reliving the past, over and over in imagination—continually criticizing himself for past mistakes—continually condemning himself for past sins."

— Maxwell Maltz

Meditation: Freedom from the past is only accomplished by your own doing. You and you alone have the choice and ability to either torture yourself for being human or forgive yourself for your humanity. This is when you will be able to live in the present moment where life exists. Forgiveness of yourself is necessary if you plan to have peace, serenity, and any form of genuine happiness. Allow yourself to escape the pain of the past and move along your course to tranquility and joyous living. It is quite senseless to continue to permit the past, which cannot be changed, to dictate your present state of living. If you feel the need to experience guilt, remorse, and regret, that's fine; however, experience it once or twice, learn the lesson intended and move on. There is no productivity in feeling this pain 147,000 times over a 30-year period.

Ask Yourself: How will you begin the process of self-forgiveness today and recognize that you did the best you could with what you had at any given time in your life?

I Affirm: Today, I will give myself permission to be free from the past and to live ecstatically in the bliss of the present moment.

JUNE 25   *"The sun will set without thy assistance."*

— The Talmud

Meditation: The Universe is so perfect when we just let it be. Everything unfolds perfectly and exactly the way it is supposed to be. Faith and connection with your higher self will guide you in the direction that you are meant to go in order to create abundance in your life. Look around, observe, and be mindful of all occurrences in each moment because they all have their special meaning and purpose as far as the life path that is specifically designed for you. All of this unfolds without you doing anything except connecting to the higher consciousness within you and believing that you will fulfill your ultimate purpose in life.

Ask Yourself: How will you allow yourself to let the Universe guide you without interfering?

I Affirm: Today, I will have faith in the power and perfection of the Universe.

JUNE 26   *"You can't build a reputation on what you're going to do."*

— Henry Ford

Meditation: Never listen to the doubts and criticism of your ego. Move forward and take the necessary steps to achieve your goals. Action is the key to success. Many individuals discuss and plan success their whole lives, but they never act upon their intentions and they are left with nothing but regret when they realize that they have procrastinated much too long. Take small but consistent steps and you will accomplish what you set out to do.

Ask Yourself: Write down something you truly want to achieve and take the first step today. If you believed you could accomplish anything, what would it be?

I Affirm: Today, I will begin taking necessary steps toward the goals I wish to achieve; I will tell myself, with confidence, that I WILL SUCCEED as long as I take consistent action.

JUNE 27 *"Great spirits have always encountered violent opposition from mediocre minds."*

— Albert Einstein

Meditation: Do not give others the power to destroy your dreams or ideals. Continue to live with your heart and soul. Human beings are often fearful of those that contemplate the truth and just in life. People are scared of change and wish to live in mediocrity and comfort. Your beliefs, your passions, and your actions may be opposed, but this will inform you that you are on the right path. Never surrender to opposition; move through it with courage and inexhaustible determination.

Ask Yourself: How will you deal with those trying to ruin your day or those trying to discourage your dreams?

I Affirm: Today, I will empathize with those individuals that have a need to live life with immense negativity; I will allow them to teach me what not to do in my life.

JUNE 28 *"Learn to be silent. Let your quiet mind listen and absorb."*

— Pythagoras

Meditation: Answers to life's questions often come to us when we reduce our analysis of life and listen to the Universe. Allow solitude and silence to enter your mind and soul today and listen to the veracity of this message. This message will offer you guidance and help you to remain on the path to successful living. Listen and you will hear the wisdom contained in the consciousness of the entire cosmos. Silence often brings insights that will solve the momentary problems of your life and direct you on your proper spiritual pathway.

Ask Yourself: Give yourself some time today and listen to what the Universe is telling you. Write down what you hear. How will you follow the universal energy rather than the material world's chaotic course?

I Affirm: Today, I will communicate with the Universe rather than unconsciously following the demands of my selfish ego.

JUNE 29 *"We cannot see, hold in our hand, or buy the things in life that truly matter."*
— Richard A. Singer, Jr.

Meditation: Honor those things that are most valuable to your heart today. I am quite positive your car, clothes, brand name shoes, or jewelry are not a part of this list. What truly gives you contentment and peace, what do you truly value in your life, and what do you truly love and possess passion for? These are the things that need to be cared for and things that you often exploit in your daily life. Step out of the illusory world and give your time and energy to what genuinely matters.

Ask Yourself: Make a list of the most important things in your life. Can you show your love and appreciation for someone or something on your list today? How will you do this?

I Affirm: Today, I will show my heart felt appreciation for the precious jewels in my life.

JUNE 30 *"I have often wondered how every man loves himself more than all the rest of men, yet sets less value on his own opinion of himself than the opinion of others."*
— Marcus Aurelius

Meditation: Begin today by honoring your feelings concerning yourself and worrying about what you want to become, not what others want you to be. Start to embrace yourself as a worthy and unique human being with unlimited possibilities in your life. Do not allow others to have power over who you are or what you become. Take back your control and live your life the way you desire to live. Strive for what you deserve and individualize your journey toward a life full of success.

Ask Yourself: Does it really matter what others think of you? If yes, why?

I Affirm: Today, I will remember that others thoughts have no power over me unless give it to them. What will be most important to me today is what I think of myself.

JULY 1

"Insanity: Doing the same thing over and over again and expecting different results."

— **Albert Einstein**

Meditation: According to this definition, 100% of all human beings inhabiting this Universe have engaged in insane behavior innumerable times. There is a very simple concept that could save the world as we know it, but, of course, let's start with ourselves. If something does not work or creates problems in your life, look for an alternative solution rather than doing the same thing over and over again. Stop insanity from ruining your life and preventing your growth. It is human to make errors in life and learn the lessons involved, but plain irrational and unproductive to keep making the same mistakes.

Ask Yourself: How will you resist insanity today? Does it help you to make the same mistakes repeatedly?

I Affirm: Today, I will make a commitment to work on changing a negative behavior that I consistently engage in.

JULY 2

"I do not look, I find."

— **Pablo Picasso**

Meditation: Discontinue your search in the external world for your pleasures and needs. Everything worthy of discovering is within the essence of your being. Once you reveal this inner treasure, you will be prepared to create a masterpiece within your life. Discover your genuine and higher self and you will truly begin to live. Set out on your inner journey each day to learn about your intrinsic gifts and grow as a spiritual and useful being that can bring extraordinary change to the world around you.

Ask Yourself: How will you search within today and discover the essence of your being?

I Affirm: Today, I will travel deep within my being and uncover the hidden gems of my soul.

JULY 3

"A tree that fills the span of a man's arms grows from a downy tip; A terrace nine stories high from handfuls of earth; A journey of a thousand miles from beneath ones feet."

— Lao-Tzu

Meditation: Great feats begin with an initial step and are created one small step at a time. Anything worth manifesting in life begins with a thought, then with specific action a little at a time. Impressive masterpieces are small works combined into greatness. Celebrated works are never fantasized and then miraculously produced; they are all a work of determination, persistence, and patience. Believe and visualize your own personal work of genius and combine with the celestial source that surrounds you to manifest it in the material world.

Ask Yourself: What will you begin today by taking the necessary small first step?

I Affirm: Today, I will ignite my inner genius and begin my masterpiece.

JULY 4

"One may go a long way after one is tired."

— French Proverb

Meditation: We can often push and persevere a long way after our mind and body informs us that we are tired and ready to resign. Follow the energy of your spirit and allow it to take over and persist in important moments. When you think you cannot go any further, go and your inner strength will carry you. It is not our mind or ego that we can rely on for persistence and perseverance, this only originates from the higher part of our being.

Ask Yourself: How will you rely on your spiritual and infinite-self today rather than concede to the limits of your corporeal being?

I Affirm: Today, I will trust in the spiritual part of my being to carry me through the day.

JULY **5**

*"I will not permit no man to narrow and degrade my soul
by making me hate him."*
— **Booker T. Washington**

Meditation: I am quite certain that there are numerous people in your life
that elicit negative emotions from you. Do not allow those individuals to have
power over you; learn from them and treat them kindly. These are the greatest
teachers you will ever encounter in life. Allow them to teach you patience and
reveal to you how you do not want to act. Silently wish them the best in their
life and advance with yours. Keep in mind that these people probably have
much more pain and suffering in their lives than you can possibly imagine.

Ask Yourself: Who can you learn from in your life today? What lessons do you
think they can teach you?

I Affirm: Today, I will honor the people in my life that provide me with great
instruction on how not to act.

JULY **6**

*"You take yourself too seriously. You are too damn important
in your own mind. That must be changed."*
— **Carlos Castaneda**

Meditation: Human beings have this innate tendency to believe their ego
when it declares, "You are the center of the Universe." Look at the larger
picture; you are one individual in an enormous human race. Individualize
your life and make some changes within. Begin to realize that you do have a
special place in this Universe, but not everything is about you or requires your
comment.

Ask Yourself: How will you internalize the fact that you are only a small piece
of the universal puzzle?

I Affirm: Today, I will live my life with purpose, but I will recognize that I am
not the purpose of life.

JULY 7

"Many persons have a wrong idea of what constitutes true happiness. It is not attained through self gratification but through fidelity to a worthy purpose."
— **Helen Keller**

Meditation: You may have noticed throughout your journey of life that to simply satisfy yourself only offers temporary pleasure, then you are back to the same place you started. This temporary sensory pleasure quickly fades into the distance and leaves us with that endless void within, that we were attempting to fill. Genuine pleasure and fulfilment of the void comes from one thing in life and that is to pursue your inner purpose and passionately do everything in your power to achieve this goal. A human being that possesses a genuine purpose in life will forever feel worthy and committed to creating meaning in the Universe.

Ask Yourself: How can you anonymously gratify someone else today? See and document the difference between gratifying someone else and gratifying yourself. Do you know what your inner purpose is in life?

I Affirm: Today, I will think of others in my life rather than focusing all of my energy on myself.

JULY 8

"Silence is the element in which great things fashion themselves together."
— **Thomas Carlyle**

Meditation: Allow yourself to sit in silence today and enjoy the peacefulness of the Universe. What is revealed to you during this silence is completely created within the Universe and not within society. The fact remains that the Universe obviously knows a bit more about truth than society. Allow your being to connect and intimately communicate with the powerful force around you and answers will be given to all your queries concerning life.

Ask Yourself: When and where will you sit and listen to the silent wisdom and suggestions of the universal force?

I Affirm: Today, I will relax and align myself with the quietude of the universal mind.

JULY **9**

"Do not be too timid and squeamish about your actions. All life is an experiment."

— **Ralph Waldo Emerson**

Meditation: Today, make a commitment not to take yourself so damn serious. Begin to experiment with your life and do the things you truly desire. Avoid doing the things that everyone else is persuading you to do and take action to make your life an adventure that satisfies your eternal self, not that of the people around you. Add adventure to your voyage and experience the exuberance that taking risks and having fun adds to your life.

Ask Yourself: What risk will you take to experiment and liven up the journey of your soul?

I Affirm: Today, I will view life as a playful adventure filled with bliss and infinite opportunities for growth.

JULY **10**

"Success is simply a matter of luck. Ask any failure."

— **Earl Wilson**

Meditation: Stop waiting for luck to sneak up on you and make your dreams come true. Step into reality and utilize your inner power to make your vision a reality. This is within your control. Luck is for those who do not have faith or hope in the miraculous force of the Universe. If you believe that all things are possible and visualize your dreams with much passion and determination, you can have anything and everything you desire.

Ask Yourself: What luck are you going to formulate in your life today?

I Affirm: Today, I will be in charge what I accomplish in my life.

JULY **11**   *"Wheresoever you go, go with all your heart."*

— Confucius

Meditation: Our heart guides us along our path through the wondrous expedition of life. To detach from your heart is to isolate yourself from what truly makes life meaningful and sacred. Living with the mind will cause much confusion and pain while living according to your heart will demonstrate who you genuinely are. Tap into the passion and love residing in your heart and express it in everything you do and everywhere you go. Doing this will make all the difference in your experience and voyage of your lifetime.

Ask Yourself: How will you live with all of your heart and soul today? Is there any reason not to live this way?

I Affirm: Today, I will immerse myself in the present moment and allow passion and love to radiate from my entire being.

JULY **12**   *"Its right to be content with what you have, but not with what you are."*

— Unknown Author

Meditation: To be content and satisfied with who you are prevents growth in all areas of your life. It is reasonable and desirable to be at peace with yourself in each waking moment of life; however, you must always persist along your path incessantly and courageously looking within and searching for areas within yourself to nurture and develop. Self-growth will transform your way of living and create a life you can only imagine. Cultivate your spiritual being and discover the personal power and the unlimited potential that inhabits your inner world.

Ask Yourself: What would you like to change about yourself today?

I Affirm: Today, I will set out to make changes in myself rather than attempting to change anyone else

JULY **13**

"The Way to Happiness: Keep your heart free from hate, your mind from worry. Live simply, expect little, give much. Fill your life with love. Scatter sunshine, forget self, think of others. Do as you would be done by. Try this for a week and you would be surprised."

— H. C. Mattern

Meditation: Hate, fear, worry, complexity, and all the other negative energies of the world impede your ability to sincerely live the life of your spirit. Why not abandon these energies starting now in your life and see what this brings. Start living simply and enjoying every moment that you are given. Give to the world, celebrate success, and enjoy an overwhelming happiness and peace in your daily walk along your journey. Try this, if you do not like it, go back to your old ways.

Ask Yourself: How will you abandon all the negative energies in order to live a genuine and spirit filled life today?

I Affirm: Today, I will follow these simple suggestions and see how I feel.

JULY **14**

"How is one to know what one can accomplish unless one tries?"

— Og Mandino

Meditation: It is quite ordinary for our human mind to tell us we cannot accomplish a goal or cannot achieve something we desire or dream of. It tells us so often that we do not deserve these great things and we are not good enough to achieve them, that we begin to truly believe and personalize these delusions. This is a combination of our lifelong development and the negative energy of our ego. The true spirit and higher self within you is not involved in this self-denigration. The secret is to tap into your inner genuis and move beyond these disparaging voices of the past.

Ask Yourself: What will you attempt to begin achieving today that your ego once demanded was impossible?

I Affirm: Today, I will refuse to pay attention to the cynical voice of my ego.

JULY 15

"Most of the things worth doing in the world had been declared impossible before they were done."
— **Louis D. Brandeis**

Meditation: Successful individuals possess two characteristics that the average person never realizes they have: they are devotion to their ultimate passions and dreams as well as determination to do whatever it takes to fulfill these. To commit to your ultimate passion and purpose in life and never give up until you accomplish it is your guarantee to success. Believe that whatever you desire is possible and never allow others to tell you differently. All great things in the Universe were once considered impossible; however, they were ultimately achieved by those who overcame the negative energy of the world and battled forward no matter what obstacle was situated in the way.

Ask Yourself: How will you turn your beliefs of the impossible into determination and passion to succeed today?

I Affirm: Today, I will believe in my ability to achieve anything I desire and I won't allow anyone in my life to discourage me.

JULY 16

"Problems are not stop signs they are guidelines."
— **Robert Schuller**

Meditation: So-called "problems" often produce unnecessary negative energy in our lives and subsequently cause us to give up halfway through our journey toward success. In the ultimate truth and reality of the Universe, this is not the purpose of problems. "Problems," or more realistically termed "challenges," are purely part of our soul's map in order to reach its destined aspiration.

Ask Yourself: How will you use challenges and difficulties in your life today as guideposts along your travels of spiritual success and evolution?

I Affirm: Today, I will think of my alleged "problems" as simply obstacles I most overcome on my way to a successful life.

JULY 17

"I find no force so devastating as the force of "cant". Within its meaning lie the roots of powerlessness. Within its vulgar four letters lies the destruction of lives: lives not lived."
— **Anonymous**

Meditation: Do not allow yourself to be a victim to the tremendous power of "can't". You can certainly do anything you desire. Break beyond the boundaries of your ego and access the power of your spirit. Within you lies the unlimited potential and ability to accomplish anything you desire. Never, let me say it one more time, NEVER allow yourself to believe the illusion and limits created around you. You, as a unique human being, establish your own personal and spiritual limits and have the faculty to accomplish anything you apply passion and determination to in your life.

Ask Yourself: How will you obliterate the boundaries of your ego today and gain access to the infinite possibilities of your essential nature?

I Affirm: Today, I will transcend my ego's restrictions and draw on the inexhaustible supply of positive energy that my spirit provides.

JULY 18

"Cultivating an active mindfulness of ones experience, moment by moment, is the path to awakening."
— **Joseph Goldstein**

Meditation: Blissful living only takes place in this precise moment. If you truly savor the moment, you will genuinely experience the reality and rapture that life has to offer. Life does not exist anywhere else but this moment, the past and the future are merely illusions of our psyche. Immerse yourself in this moment right now and awaken the ecstasy that patiently waits within you. Wake up and live today.

Ask Yourself: How will you thoroughly experience the present moment in your life today?

I Affirm: Today, I will completely surrender to the present, rather than trying to live in the illusions of the past and future.

JULY **19**

*"The search for comfort through sense pleasures
rarely has an end."*

— Mark Epstein, M.D.

Meditation: We are free to choose to travel through our lives seeking pleasure from cars, clothes, electronics, jewelry, and, of course, substances and the almighty dollar . However, rarely has a person truly obtained happiness from any of these peripheral things, in fact I will venture to say this has never been accomplished. This search in the external world is an incessant journey with an uncomfortable conclusion; it never allows genuine heartfelt contentment or peace. This chase is filled with suffering and frustration and goes on eternally unless an intrinsic commitment is made to search within for soul-felt happiness and serenity.

Ask Yourself: What will make you genuinely happy today?

I Affirm: Today, I will abandon my useless search for pleasure in the external world and explore the inherent bliss that resides within my soul.

JULY **20**

"Problems are messages."

— Shakti Gawain

Meditation: Eliminate the word "problem" from your vocabulary and you will prevent the presence of unnecessary negative energy in your life. Without so-called "problems," we do not learn to grow, mature, or evolve as human beings. "Problems" are merely pieces of the puzzle that we must rotate and find a place for in the larger portrait of life. Successful and peaceful living comes from embracing challenges and following the guidance they provide for you upon your passage to abundance.

Ask Yourself: How will you embrace "problems" in order to grow and evolve today?

I Affirm: Today, I will cease labeling challenges in my life as "problems" and more realistically see them as opportunities for advancement in life.

JULY **21**

*"Men who succeed keep open minds
and are afraid of nothing."*
— **Napoleon Hill**

Meditation: Fear and a closed mind will certainly create a mundane and spiritless existence. When you allow your ego to dominate your life you merely exist and give up your opportunity to thoroughly enjoy life. It is a vital task to continuously keep your mind open to all possibilities and to prevent fear from controlling the way you travel along your path to success. Fear is merely an indication that you are on your way to a better way of living. Remain open to everything the Universe has to offer you and extinguish fear from your life.

Ask Yourself: What will you do today to confront fear and break through the boundaries of your restrictive ego?

I Affirm: Today, I will remain open to the vast opportunities that the Universe offers me.

JULY **22**

"Whosoever is willing to lose his ego will find his soul."
— **M. Scott Peck**

Meditation: Our ego separates us from the universal spirit and pervasive consciousness. It denies and desires to eliminate the connection that consists within everyone and everything in the cosmos. If we are to connect with the eternal and enlightened, we must begin decreasing the power and effects of the ego on our life. Your ego wants nothing but to cause you suffering, pain, separation, and chaos. It disconnects your being from the ultimate reality and oneness of humanity. Reconnect to the universal source and take pleasure in the euphoria of unity and peace.

Ask Yourself: How will you begin to let go of the delusions of the ego?

I Affirm: Today, I will follow the luminosity of my spirit rather than the darkness of my ego.

July

JULY **23**

"The best use of life is to spend it on something that outlasts life."

— **William James**

Meditation: We were created as unique architects in charge of the universal blueprint. All human beings are here to contribute something for the advancement of humanity. During our brief stay, we are free to make choices; however, ultimately, we have a specific responsibility to accomplish. Rather than focusing on temporary pleasures of the physical world, discover what you can do to add to the development of creation and what you can contribute to the eternal advancement of the Universe.

Ask Yourself: How will you discover your ultimate mission in the world and what are you going to do to begin making progress on this today?

I Affirm: Today, I will contemplate what I can leave behind for the use of humanity when I pass on to the spiritual realm.

JULY **24**

"Laundry is the only thing that should be separated by color."

— **Unknown Author**

Meditation: Separation of human beings by any characteristic is complete idiocy and absolute insanity. Diversity and variation make this world extraordinary and gives us an opportunity to grow spiritually and unite as one race. Remember, there is only one race and that consists of all humanity. If humanity is to prosper and thrive in the future, we must get rid of this ridiculous idea that any human being is inferior based on external characteristics such as race, ethnicity, religion, creed, and all the other aspects we use to rationalize exclusivity.

Ask Yourself: Do you possess prejudicial beliefs or biased judgments regarding people who appear different from you? Do you plan to continue this nonsense?

I Affirm: Today, I will explore my beliefs about the nature of humanity and challenge any irrational or nonsensical beliefs.

Your Daily Walk with the Great Minds | 123

JULY **25**

"Shoot for the moon, even if you miss you'll land among the stars."

— Les Brown

Meditation: Mediocrity seems to be a dis-ease of the ego. So many individuals are accepting of merely being average. We are not here to be average; we have an extraordinary journey to take part in and need to begin moving along that path. Move away from the bonds of the ego and utilize your impressive ability to achieve all that you desire in your life. Did you dream of mediocrity, boredom, and conformity as a child? Then do not do it now. Get out of this rut of monotony and comfort and begin achieving excellence in everything you do.

Ask Yourself: How will you move away from mediocrity and begin achieving greatness today?

I Affirm: Today, I will leave the security of my comfort zone and take a risk.

JULY **26**

"Success seems to be largely a matter of hanging on after others have let go."

— William Feathers

Meditation: Continue on the journey toward your goals and your deepest desires and do not give up before the miracle happens. It may be just around the corner. Make a commitment to always go beyond what you are expected to do. Do not limit your beliefs concerning the possibilities you are capable of. Make it a point to continuously express to yourself that you were programmed for extraordinary success and you will not resign until you achieve it.

Ask Yourself: What do you feel like giving up on today and how are you going to hang on and push yourself the extra mile?

I Affirm: Today, I will repeat to myself the following statement, "I am programmed for extraordinary success."

JULY **27**

"There isn't a person anywhere who isn't capable of doing more than he thinks he can."

— Henry Ford

Meditation: We tend to doubt our abilities and question our talents. It seems to be a facet of the human condition. However, men and women throughout history have shown us clearly that greatness is possible. These notable human beings overcame their doubts and were persistent in their struggle for success. These individuals were no different than you, they just believed they were special and they went ahead and manifested phenomenal achievements in their lives. You are truly just as capable as these great human beings; it's simply a matter of believing in yourself and going to get what you desire in life.

Ask Yourself: What will you do today that you once believed was impossible?

I Affirm: Today, I will remember that impossibility is a frame of mind not a reality.

JULY **28**

"The easiest thing to find on God's green earth is someone to tell you all the things you cannot do."

— Richard M. Demos

Meditation: Many human beings that surround us in our lives feel horrible about themselves and have little belief in their ability to achieve anything worthwhile. This is unfortunate that they live this way; however, it is unnecessary to allow these individuals to poison you with negative energy and pessimism. Start surrounding yourself with people who support and encourage your dreams. Simply say thank you to those who attempt to tell you what you can and cannot do. Eventually, you may be able to act as a role model to these negatively energized beings and teach them that the impossible is actually possible.

Ask Yourself: Who will you converse with today that will encourage you to live and create your dreams? Who will you encourage and support today to live and create their dreams?

I Affirm: Today, I will encourage myself in everything I do. I will also encourage others to pursue their dreams.

JULY 29   *"No one can make you feel inferior without your consent."*
— **Eleanor Roosevelt**

Meditation: There are many individuals that walk this earth believing and acting as if they are better than or smarter than others, however, the fact will always remain that we are all equal human beings. Simply enjoy your life today amongst the entire human race and never allow another individual to have power over who you are and what you become. Believe in yourself as a worthwhile and special human being and discard the poisonous energy directed toward you from other individuals who obviously doubt themselves and their worthiness in humanity.

Ask Yourself: Do you believe you are better than any other human being? If so, how do you plan to begin living the truth today and accept yourself as an equal part of humanity? Do you believe others are superior to you? What is wrong with you as a person that allows this faulty and irrational belief to contaminate part of your precious being?

I Affirm: Today, I will enjoy being me.

JULY 30   *"It's a funny thing about life; if you refuse to accept anything but the best, you very often get it."*
— **W. Somerset Maugham**

Meditation: Doing the best in our life is very simple. It consists of making our mind up that we have the ability to accomplish our dreams and desires and not giving up until we achieve excellence in everything we do. We continue on with determination and persistence in spite of all difficulties and never , ever, ever give up. These characteristics and mindset are what make human beings great and allows them to surpass the mediocrity accepted in the society around us.

Ask Yourself: How will you set your heart and soul on nothing but excellence today?

I Affirm: Today, I will set my sights on superior achievement , rather than settling for anything less.

126 | *Your Daily Walk with the Great Minds*

JULY **31**

"In matters of style swim with the current, on matters of principle stand like a rock."

— **Thomas Jefferson**

Meditation: There are many aspects of life that can simply be accepted and dealt with by going with the flow, on the other hand, when it comes to the principles of your being, you must stand strong and never back down. The world around you will try to defeat you, however, your job is to reach inside and tap into your inner spirit and hold on. Keep your foundation beneath you and never compromise your values.

Ask Yourself: How will you stand firm and protect your cherished personal principles?

I Affirm: Today, I will compose a list that describes my most precious values and principles; I will decide if I am sincerely living according to these essential elements of my being..

AUGUST 1   *"Don't find fault. Find a remedy."*

— Henry Ford

Meditation: It is quite possible to find negativity in everything we encounter in our life. If we are constantly looking for the negative aspects of life we will certainly discover them. Instead of focusing on the negative or the "problem," try focusing on the positive in situations and seeking solutions and creative ways of improving the circumstances. One of the most important strategies in life is to seek the positive in everything around you and create solutions that lead to growth and advancement in your life, rather than allowing the negative aspect of your mind to take over and color everything with a despairing tint.

Ask Yourself: How will you keep your focus on the positive that pervades the Universe and seek solutions rather than seeking someone or something to blame?

I Affirm: Today, I will keep my mind, body, and soul aligned with the positive energy of the Universe.

⊰━◉ ◉━⊱

AUGUST 2   *"The mind is its own place, and in it self can make a heaven a hell, a hell a heaven."*

— John Molton

Meditation: Our mind united with our soul is our most potent resource. We can choose to be peaceful in the most intense chaos or chaotic in absolute peace. We have control of more than we can ever imagine. Reality is fashioned within us and we can create the reality that will help us succeed in life or create the reality that can enable us to become complete failures. Utilize your inner resources to create the life you want and the life your heart and soul desire.

Ask Yourself: How will you utilize your internal power today in order to create the life you were born to live?

I Affirm: Today, I will utilize the capacity of my inner resources to manifest absolute tranquility and joy in my life.

AUGUST 3
"Where do you live?"
"Young people live in the future."
"Old people live in the past"
"Wise people live in the present."

— **Unknown Author**

Meditation: Do you constantly dwell on the mistakes of the past, the regrets, and the emotional turmoil, or do you drown yourself in the worries and the dread of the future? The only place that life can truly be enjoyed is in the now. If you are in the past or the future, you are throwing away the precious experiences of life and merely existing. The choice of when and where you live is of course yours; however, if you desire peace, serenity, and contentment, the only place that has this available to you is right now in this present moment.

Ask Yourself: Would you please join life today and dance in the illumination and enlightenment of this precise moment?

I Affirm: Today, I will perform an experiment: I will wholeheartedly engross myself in the present moment without descending into the past or projecting myself into the future. See how your day unfolds and compare it to the way you usually exist.

AUGUST 4
"He that waits upon fortune is never sure of a dinner."

— **Benjamin Franklin**

Meditation: Be sure never to count on wealth, success, or even happiness to come upon you unexpectedly and free of charge. Get out and commit yourself to your ultimate purpose and remain determined to achieve and you will then discover the fortune that awaits you. No matter what you crave in life, if you remain passionate and persevere you will slowly but surely achieve excellence.

Ask Yourself: How will you get out and claim what is yours today?

I Affirm: Today, I will work diligently for the success that is mine.

AUGUST **5**   *"The quality of a person's life is in direct proportion to their commitment to excellence, regardless of their chosen field of endeavor."*

— Vincent Lombardi

Meditation: Whatever it is you do, the secret of success and a fulfiling and adventurous life is to consistently pursue your purpose with courageous determination, intense passion, and interminable persistence. If you do this, you will certainly contribute honorable and noble advancements to the Universe. No matter what it is you choose to pursue in your life, believe that you will be great at it and this will become a reality. Greatness is encoded in every element of your being.

Ask Yourself: Today, how will you follow the above-mentioned recipe for success and never relinquish your personal power to create excellence along your path?

I Affirm: Today, I will remind myself that often that, "Greatness is encoded in every element of my being."

AUGUST **6**   *"We make a living by what we get; we make a life by what we give."*

— Winston Churchill

Meditation: Countless times throughout our lives, we allow our ego to take over and delude us into thinking that what we earn monetarily, materialistically, and physically is what defines us as human beings. However, if you truly take a sincere look at your life and what plays an important role in it, you will most certainly prove your ego wrong. Contributing the love and compassion that lives within your heart to humanity will certainly give you genuine worth much quicker and longer than what you get out of life.

Ask Yourself: How will you remain conscious of what is genuinely important in your life today?

I Affirm: Today, I will recognize that material possessions are temporary, but offerings from the heart are eternal.

AUGUST 7 *"Adopt the pace of nature; her secret is patience."*

— Ralph Waldo Emerson

Meditation: The Universe often comes together for us when we practice patience and allow nature to figure things out in our life. We often profess that we have all the correct answers; however, allow yourself to believe in the creative energy of life today rather than your own mind and see the results for yourself. Remember this in the future when you are trying to come up with all the answers and think that you know it all. We are not omnipotent, but the Universe sure the is. Trust it and reap the immense benefits that lie before you.

Ask Yourself: How will you surrender yourself to the universal intelligence today and keep your hands out of this important work?

I Affirm: Today, I will trust in the brilliance of the Universe and release myself from the illusion of control.

AUGUST 8 *"Nothing is particularly hard if you divide it into small jobs."*

— Henry Ford

Meditation: If you look at the total picture of any goal or task in your life, it appears to be tremendously overwhelming and almost impossible to accomplish. Instead of provoking this unnecessary anxiety in your life give yourself a break and take small manageable and easily accomplished steps toward the end result you desire.

Ask Yourself: What will you break into small steps today and commence working on?

I Affirm: Today, I will begin building the foundation of my success one small step a time.

AUGUST **9** *"Blessed is the influence of one true loving human soul on another."*

— **George Eliot**

Meditation: Envision a world where the central purpose of human beings is to help their fellow human beings. That would be a world of peace and pure bliss. This can be a reality if we begin this goal within ourselves and our community. Lend a hand to your fellow members of humanity and act with genuine kindness toward all beings. Doing this will bring immense satisfaction to your heart and will in turn make an immeasurable difference in the transformation of the Universe.

Ask Yourself: What will you do to help another human being today?

I Affirm: Today, I will embark on the most important task of my life; to help another human being simply for the purpose of helping a fellow traveler of life.

AUGUST **10** *"All that you accomplish or fail to accomplish with your life is the direct result of your thoughts."*

— **James Allen**

Meditation: Today, focus entirely on your thoughts. Think big, think abundance, think successful, and think completely affirming thoughts. Anytime your ego desires to initiate a negative thought process, immediately stop the process and replace it with a positive one. All of our successes or failures are manufactured beginning with our thoughts. You can choose to think, believe, and visualize extraordinary accomplishment or immense failure. It all comes down to what you believe and tell yourself during your inner conversations. Visualize and believe in what you desire in your life and you will create it.

Ask Yourself: What will your positive thought mantra be today? What does success in your life look like?

I Affirm: Today, I will stand guard at the gates of my mind and only allow positive thoughts to enter.

AUGUST **11** *"Many of life's failures are people who did not realize how close they were to success when they gave up."*
— **Thomas Edison**

Meditation: Never surrender in the face of challenges. Challenges are just the Universe's way of making sure you earn and deserve the success you are striving for. If you work vigorously with persistence and dedication while connecting to the force that surrounds you, destiny will provide you with the attainment of your desire. You must keep moving and tackling the problems that are thrown your way and when the Universe is convinced you are ready for success, it will be given to you. This readiness assessed by the Universe has to do with learning the lessons you were intended to learn along the way.

Ask Yourself: How will you keep yourself from giving up on your goals?

I Affirm: Today, I will unite with the energy of the Universe and follow my dream and desires to completion.

AUGUST **12** *"There is only one success—*
to be able to spend your life in your own way."
— **Christopher Morley**

Meditation: Individual success is defined based on your unique goals, desires, and dreams. In addition, success in your life is linked to the ultimate purpose you were brought here to pursue. If you are able to realize these yearnings no matter what they are, you are successful. Always trust in yourself and your ability to follow the guidance of your inner genius. Rid yourself of the resistance created by your ego and follow what your soul suggests. Spending your life in your own way refers to spending your life free of societal and ego based demands. It is living your life the way your genuine-self desires.

Ask Yourself: How will you take the first step toward pleasing your pure self?

I Affirm: Today, I will enter my inner world and search intently for the purpose that I was specifically created to fulfill.

AUGUST **13** *"Greater is he who acts from love than he who acts from fear."*

— Simeon Ben Eleazar

Meditation: The Universe and the powerful energy of love unite as one perfect force. They are one and the same. The cosmos is made and functions based on unconditional love. Where there is love there is spirituality. Where there is love there is growth. Where there is love there are infinite possibilities. Attach to the love contained in the luminous energy that surrounds you and you will radiate this eternal force in all your thoughts, beliefs, actions, and expressions. Love yourself, love others, and love the world around you. Love is the essence of life. Love is the answer to all problems.

Ask Yourself: How will you live your day overflowing with love?

I Affirm: Today, I will take a risk and express my love for someone special in my life.

AUGUST **14** *"Worry often gives a small thing a big shadow."*

— Swedish Proverb

Meditation: A vast amount of human beings destroy precious moments throughout their lives due to unnecessary worry. The important thing to realize is the fact that worry does absolutely nothing productive for the past, present, or future. Why continue to do something over and over again that is completely unproductive and actually quite unhealthy. Would you walk out of your house and begin digging a whole without a purpose or reason for doing so? Continuing to dig and dig after blisters form on your hands and your energy is being depleted for no apparent reason. Hours, days, and months go by and you continue to dig with no productive or logical reasoning. Hopefully, you would not do this, so why do you continue to worry?

Ask Yourself: What can you be accomplishing if you were not wasting so much time worrying? How much better would you feel about life?

I Affirm: Today, I will put aside all my worries until the end of the day, then I will give myself a half hour to worry as much as I desire.

AUGUST **15** *"There is a rhythm to the Universe. When we are able to get quiet enough, we experience how we are part of that perfect rhythm."*

— **Dr. Wayne Dyer**

Meditation: Connect and participate in the magnificent orchestra of life. You have a special place in this symphony, which can only be discovered by quieting your mind and connecting to the precise pulse of the Universe. This rhythm exists outside of your understanding and intellect and can only be connected to by detaching from your ego and relying on the invisible force of the cosmos. This silent and unseen force connects everything and everyone we come into contact with. Connecting and perfecting your association with this power will allow you to achieve anything you wish without being interrupted by anything that stands in your way.

Ask Yourself: How will you quiet your mind today and tune into the rhythm of life?

I Affirm: Today, I will silent my mind and allow my soul to be absorbed by rhythm of the universe.

AUGUST **16** *"Mans main task in life is to give birth to himself, to become what he potentially is."*

— **Erich Fromm**

Meditation: We are born to this world with a genuine seed of perfection within us. Whether we choose to cultivate and nurture our inner life is our ultimate choice. You can become what others and society tell you to become or you can blossom into the perfect spirit you were meant to be. We all have a perfect design for our life deep within us, the problem is we disconnect from this plan and follow the ego's way. Our true purpose and design for living can only be achieved by reconnecting to the higher force within us and following its guidance meticulously.

Ask Yourself: Will you choose to allow society to prepare or charter your destiny or will you follow your internal design?

I Affirm: Today, I will embark on the most important journey of my life; discovering and manifesting my genuine self.

AUGUST **17** *"Patience and time do more than strength or passion."*

— Jean De La Fontaine

Meditation: Continue to persevere on the path toward your dreams and desires; however, it is imperative to listen to the Universe when it tells you to wait and take a break. Connect with the force of the spirit rather than the force of the ego; the influence of the spirit always overcomes the lower energy of the ego. Do not push when the Universe tells you to slow down, listen and heed the advice of this infinite power.

Ask Yourself: How will you practice patience and relaxation today?

I Affirm: Today, I will tune into the quiet expression of the Universe, rather than following the noise and demands of the ego.

AUGUST **18** *"The only way to deal with the future is to function efficiently in the now."*

— Gita Bellin

Meditation: As a separate reality, the future does not exist, thus we can truly do nothing about it. However, I must exclaim that the current moments of your life do merge to produce what your future becomes. The process of achieving excellence in the NOW sets the flow in your life to arrive at future excellence. Right now, right here in this moment is the only way to create what you desire for yourself in the future. Live now, achieve now, and experience the exhilaration of the present moment to the fullest. Immersion in the ocean of now will allow your life to flow with the harmony of the Universe.

Ask Yourself: How can you begin building the future you desire in this very moment?

I Affirm: Today, I will indulge in the bliss and excitement of the NOW.

AUGUST **19** *"There is more to life than increasing its speed."*

— M. K. Gandhi

Meditation: Life tends to speed up each and everyday that passes. The goal of society appears to be getting things done as expeditious as possible and then to move on to the next monotonous meaningless task. We run around doing, doing, doing. Life is more than merely getting things done as fast as possible and eliminating your inexhaustible to do list. Embrace and honor that which is precious in your life today and eliminate society's useless need for speed.

Ask Yourself: How will you stop and cherish the humanity around you today and bask in the glow of life's blissful journey?

I Affirm: Today, I will awaken to the tranquility contained in each and every moment and cease living according to society's anxiety filled pace.

AUGUST **20** *"Life is a field of unlimited possibilities."*

— Deepak Chopra

Meditation: Escape the boundaries of the physical and material in your life today and access the boundless and infinite universal power. If you access this source, you will cease to have limits in your life and will have the freedom to manifest anything you desire. Everything you want, everything you aspire to be, and everything your soul desires is within your being. The task is to reach within and transform this intrinsic energy to your outside world.

Ask Yourself: How will you gain access to this unlimited field of opportunities today?

I Affirm: Today, I will recognize that all of my limits are self created and I can transcend these limits any time I choose.

AUGUST **21** *"Let us so live that when we die even the undertaker will be sorry."*

— **Mark Twain**

Meditation: Live your life according to the guidance of your higher self and you will surely be an inspiration to all human beings you come into contact with. Allow the intuition of your soul to guide you to higher states of consciousness and become a role model for spiritual living. Let the love, compassion, and kindness exude from your being and touch all those you meet. This is the authentic purpose of your soul, allow this purpose to be discovered and absorbed by all.

Ask Yourself: How do you plan on following your inner guidance today and expressing your love to all beings?

I Affirm: Today, I will allow the rays of my soul to shine upon all of humanity.

AUGUST **22** *"Become addicted to constant and never ending self improvement."*

— **Anthony J. D'Angelo**

Meditation: Addiction to impermanent and fleeting pleasures has slowly taken over this Universe and is the primary reason for the breakdown of many societies. Human beings often believe they are treating themselves well when they choose to ease their mind with drugs, alcohol, television, or any other wavering self-gratification technique. Today, begin your addiction to improving and evolving as a spiritual being rather than engrossing yourself in harmful and destructive transient pleasures.

Ask Yourself: How will you begin your positive addiction to self-improvement and growth today?

I Affirm: Today, I will begin my journey toward greater self awareness and spiritual advancement.

AUGUST 23 *"Strength lies in differences not in similarities."*
— **Stephen Covey**

Meditation: Diversity throughout the world, in human beings, and in all the creatures that inhabit this earth make life fascinating, fulfilling, and enlightening. Rather than fearing differences and excluding diverse populations from your life, make it your life education to learn and embrace the differences that are contained in this miraculous Universe.

Ask Yourself: How will you honor and learn about diversity in the world today?

I Affirm: Today, I will embrace the variety of the human race rather than enclosing myself in a box filled with people just like me.

AUGUST 24 *"We find no real satisfaction in life without obstacles to conquer and goals to achieve."*
— **Maxwell Maltz**

Meditation: The universal spirit combined with your heart and soul's desire will stop at nothing but abundance and complete serenity in your life. Apply the power of these internal and infinite resources to endure and accomplish the goals you crave to manifest in your life. Enjoy the educational journey and allow yourself to grow and develop along the way. Obstacles and challenges are your allies along this process of advancement.

Ask Yourself: How will you apply this force today to accomplish the goals and dreams that you desire?

I Affirm: Today, I will recognize the value of obstacles in my life as predestined lessons designed for my spiritual evolution.

AUGUST 25 *"Two roads diverged in a yellow wood, and I—I took the one less traveled by, and that has made all the difference."*
— **Robert Frost**

Meditation: Do not simply follow the guiding principles defined by society and all of its institutions. Access what lies in your soul and dare to walk and create your own path on your personal journey of life. Conforming to the mediocrity and monotony of life stunts your personal and spiritual growth and does not allow you to access your innate creativity and uniqueness. Activating originality and imagination in your life will allow you to play a fundamental role in the innovative transformation of the world. Take your own path, and I can assure you that this decision will make all the difference in the results you generate in your life.

Ask Yourself: What path will you begin to create today?

I Affirm: Today, I will escape conformity and travel my own creative path.

AUGUST 26 *"I cried because I had no shoes until I saw man who had no feet."*
— **Unknown Author**

Meditation: At times in our lives, we lack gratitude for the things that we have, the abilities we possess, and the people in our lives that provide unconditional love and support. Our egos are always demanding more and more, always postponing happiness, and always thinking we have it bad or that life is not being fair to us. It often helps to contemplate and ponder those individuals throughout the world that are much less fortunate than ourselves and that actually suffer to survive physically on a daily basis. There is always someone worse off than you. Gratitude can often allow you to appreciate the beauty and gifts in your own life.

Ask Yourself: What are you truly grateful for today? If you think you are broken and in poverty, add up the value of the things you have. How much would you sell your children for, your eyesight, the love of the people around you, your legs, your hearing, etc? Write down your value!

I Affirm: Today, I will honestly assess the true value of my life and focus on appreciation rather than self pity.

AUGUST **27** *"You nourish your soul by fulfiling your destiny."*

— Harold Kushner

Meditation: We have two paths we can choose in our lives. The one we are directed to take by those around us and society in general or the one we are intended to travel according to our soul's purpose. You are born with an innate purpose and design for living. Throughout your development and interaction with society, this purpose is carelessly buried by false beliefs and the ego's endless demands and criticisms. Begin cleansing your internal world and unearthing this ultimate purpose. Once you have discovered it, the Universe will guide you in the process of actualizing it in your life.

Ask Yourself: Are you being misguided by society or are you following your soul's code? What is your soul's ultimate purpose for your life?

I Affirm: Today, I will feed my soul by aligning with my purpose.

AUGUST **28** *"Success demands singleness of purpose."*

— Vincent Lombardi

Meditation: Do you have a purpose in your life or are you just merely keeping busy with the monotony of daily living? Do you know why you are here? What gives meaning to your life? If you have discovered your purpose, congratulations. If not, dig down to the depths of your soul and seek the purpose of your being. This may take some intense cleaning and digging, put rest assured your purpose and specific design for living resides within you.

Ask Yourself: How can you begin the internal search for your ultimate purpose today? If you have already found your purpose, how will you step up the pace and progress forward in your pursuit?

I Affirm: Today, I will live with purpose and meaning, instead of constantly pursuing external possessions.

AUGUST **29** *"Formal education will make you a living; self education will make you a fortune."*

— **Jim Rohn**

Meditation: Educational institutions are a wonderful facet of our lives; however, they are only one aspect of our collective educational experience. Throw yourself into life and experience the education of existence, love, challenge, and all the other enlightening opportunities available in this vast Universe. Your entire life is an intense learning experience and with each new lesson comes more wisdom and the potential to know who you truly are, how to sincerely live, and to how discern what is valuable and worthwhile and what is senseless and petty. Enjoy the learning experience and most importantly always remain an open minded and willing student of the Universe.

Ask Yourself: How will you receive valuable education from life today?

I Affirm: Today, I will live each moment with vigilance and be on the look out for significant learning experiences presented by the Universe.

AUGUST **30** *"In the middle of difficulty lies opportunity."*

— **Albert Einstein**

Meditation: Do you truly desire to be free from difficulties and challenges in your life? With challenges and difficulties come growth, joy, and the experience of triumph. Without difficult moments, life would be quite tedious and meaningless. Embrace the challenges that are presented to you in life and learn the lessons that the Universe is imparting to you. Utilize this universal wisdom in your journey of internal development.

Ask Yourself: How will you embrace and learn a lesson from each difficulty that arises in your passage through life today?

I Affirm: Today, I will take advantage of the tremendous opportunities that are hidden in each challenge I face.

AUGUST **31** *"To be alive is to love. Those who live the most dangerously, creatively, and wonderfully are the great lovers in the world."*

— **Father William McNamara**

Meditation: Take risks, live adventurously, love your fellow human beings, and create the exhilarating life you have always imagined. Remember, life is a rehearsal for eternity so you had better make the most of it. Express your love in every act of living you are involved in. Love is what keeps the world alive and love is what will transform the Universe, as we know it. Love is the overwhelming force that connects all things and beings that exist in this world. Love has the power to change the cosmos.

Ask Yourself: How will you genuinely and adventurously live today?

I Affirm: Today, I will creatively express my innate and powerful capacity to love.

Your Daily Walk with the Great Minds | *143*

SEPTEMBER 1 *"Believe when you are most unhappy, that there is something for you to do in the world. So long as you can sweeten another's pain, life is not in vain."*

— **Helen Keller**

Meditation: When we live life according to our essential purpose, there is no reason to enter a state of discontent. We know that we are adding to the Universe and will transform the world in our own unique and special way. Adding to humanity and the betterment of the world is a life-long journey that always brings us contentment and equanimity knowing that we are living for a cause rather than living a meaningless and selfish existence.

Ask Yourself: How will you add to humanity today and begin or continue making a difference in the world?

I Affirm: Today, I will share my life with another human being.

SEPTEMBER 2 *"The cynic says "One man can't do anything."*

— **John Gardner**

Meditation: Make sure to challenge the venomous energy and the cynicism of the ego whenever it provokes you to believe or even entertain the thought that you "can't" do something. Make sure you remind yourself of the reality that you live in a Universe with endless possibilities and that you can accomplish anything you desire as long as all your heart and soul is passionate and engaged in it. Detach yourself from pessimism and always remember within you lies infinite potential.

Ask Yourself: What will you do today or begin today that your ego once told you that you "can't" accomplish?

I Affirm: Today, I will not believe the illusion that my ego is me; I will believe what is ultimately true, that I am a spiritual being with no limits.

SEPTEMBER 3 *"If you have much, give of your wealth, if you have little give of your heart."*

— **Arabian Proverb**

Meditation: Live a life of benevolence and you will receive immense spiritual rewards. Live a life of simply receiving and you have wasted the robust generosity of your being. Give everything you can and your life will undeniably be filled with abundance. This is the spiritual law of humanity. We must give all of what we have to offer in order to receive the gifts of the world. Giving monetarily is a gracious gesture, but the ultimate gift is giving of your time, energy, compassion, and kindness.

Ask Yourself: What will you give today and who will you give it to?

I Affirm: Today, I will truly experience the divine bliss that life contains by giving directly from my heart.

SEPTEMBER 4 *"Life's most urgent question is what are you doing for others?"*

— **Dr. Martin Luther King, Jr.**

Meditation: Liberation from suffering comes only from kindness to the human race and the willingness to make a difference in other human being's lives. This is to be done no matter what society says. Our ego and the world around us often attaches to the faulty beliefs related to what the world can give to you or what you can take from the world. Although the essential question in life is what you can contribute to the world. This is what is sacred in our lives, what we leave the world as a contribution from our soul.

Ask Yourself: What will you do to enhance humanity today?

I Affirm: Today, I will expend all my energy helping others.

SEPTEMBER **5** *"Never talk defeat. Use words like hope, belief, faith, and victory."*

— **Norman Vincent Peale**

Meditation: Thinking or talking about defeat in your life will certainly program you for failure. Why not decide to constantly think or talk about success and give yourself a chance in life? It obviously cannot hurt since you will be thinking and talking anyway. Program your being to seek the abundance and success that surrounds you. Use your words to guide your entire being toward the wishes you would like to be granted in your life. Words are a powerful, emotive, and influential component of our lives, if we use them correctly our lives, relationships, and desires will all be exactly the way we program them to be.

Ask Yourself: What is your plan to program your being for continuous success today?

I Affirm: Today, I will think, believe, talk and visualize success in everything I do.

SEPTEMBER **6** *"Whatever you can do, or dream you can, begin it. Boldness has genius, power and magic in it. Begin it now."*
— **Goethe**

Meditation: There is no difference between you and all the other exceptional individuals throughout history that have achieved their greatest dreams and created the lives they imagined only in their slumber. You have this embryonic genius within you that is waiting to be born and waiting to give birth to a transformation in your life and the world you inhabit. You have miracles housed within your being and it is now time to reveal them and unleash them into the Universe.

Ask Yourself: What is your dream and how will you begin to make it a reality today?

I Affirm: Today, I will believe in miracles and begin working toward one RIGHT NOW.

SEPTEMBER 7 *"Be at peace and see a clear pattern and plan running through your lives. Nothing is by chance."*
— Eileen Caddy

Meditation: Be mindful of the clues and pieces of your individual puzzle that are presented along your journey by the universal force. Everywhere around you, things are happening that fit in perfectly to your purpose and design here on earth. Look around and know that the Universe is guiding you along your path to eternal success and ultimate purpose. You can make a choice to remain connected to the force that devised this plan or you can try your ego's plan.

Ask Yourself: How will you utilize these clues today in your pursuit of success and contentment?

I Affirm: Today, I will remain aware each precious moment, so I will be alert to the secret language of the Universe.

SEPTEMBER 8 *"Confine yourself to the present."*

— Marcus Aurelius

Meditation: This may be the secret we have been longing for since the beginning of time. This one principle, if followed and practiced, will give you the peace and tranquility you desire in your life. Begin living wholeheartedly in the present moment. Remember, you are always in the now; this is all you have control of. All the gifts and signs that the Universe has for you are presented right in this moment. Connection to life and the precious offerings are only available in the present. Listen, learn, enjoy, and find peace in this very moment. This is the secret that most human beings never benefit from due to their ego's obsession to change the past and control the future.

Ask Yourself: What is your plan to begin applying this secret of life to your daily existence?

I Affirm: Today, I will refuse to spoil the present moment by regretting the past and agonizing about the future.

SEPTEMBER **9** *"Who looks outside dreams. Who looks inside wakes."*

— **Carl Jung**

Meditation: To explore within your entire being allows you to grow and evolve as a unique spiritual entity. Inner examination will eventually lead to the evolution and enlightenment of your spirit. Society and our ego often believe that peace and pleasure are found in the external world; this is the greatest fallacy of living. We can only nurture our being by looking within and relying on our internal resources to guide us toward the success we desire in life. Dive into the depths of your being and realize the remarkable wealth that is available to direct your path in life.

Ask Yourself: How will you make a commitment to begin searching within in order for your life to evolve?

I Affirm: Today, I will awake from the destructive dreams of the ego and align with the divine awareness present within my genuine self.

SEPTEMBER **10** *"Everyone and everything around you is your teacher."*

— **Ken Keyes, Jr.**

Meditation: Life is always a stimulating learning experience. It is our responsibility to look at life as an educational opportunity and learn whatever we can to grow and evolve physically, mentally, emotionally, and spiritually. Every human being we come into contact with provides us with information concerning our life's lessons and we do the same for others. We are connected to one silent and omnipresent force that links us to the specific learning experiences that we need to advance and develop in this Universe. Never pass up a transformative experience by prejudging it as insignificant or inconsequential. Make learning your number one priority in your unique journey.

Ask Yourself: Look within and see what you can discover about yourself today?

I Affirm: Today, I will remember that everyone I see, speak to, and encounter today has something essential to teach me, this is the connection and the unity that exists within all beings.

SEPTEMBER **11**

September

"I am looking for a lot of men that have an infinite capacity to not know what can't be done."
— **Henry Ford**

Meditation: Anything in this vast Universe is possible. Do not allow anyone to tell you differently. If everyone doubted their ability to accomplish their dreams we would have no automobiles, no aircraft, no electricity, no computers and we would still believe that the world was flat. Connect to the immense power of the celestial force and realize how much in life is actually achievable and within your reach. Tap into your vibrant energy center and set yourself up for greatness. Always remain conscious of the fact that limits, boundaries, "cant's," impossibilities, and restrictions are all part of your finite ego and have nothing to do with the truth of the boundless cosmos.

Ask Yourself: What action will you take today in order to prove to yourself that achievement of your goals is possible and actually within your control?

I Affirm: Today, I will believe in myself as a capable and worthy human being.

SEPTEMBER **12**

"Do not lose your inward peace for anything whatsoever, even if your whole world seems upset."
— **Saint Francis De Sales**

Meditation: The secret to peace and serenity is to maintain your inner calmness no matter what is going on in your external world. Always be assured that no matter what goes on in life around you, everything will be okay within you. The true power of life resides within your being and can either be dictated by you or you can allow the world around you to hold the power. Freedom of peace and tranquility is born within you and then will emanate from your being to attract what and who you desire in your life.

Ask Yourself: How will you create and maintain inner peace in your life today?

I Affirm: Today, I will refuse to engage in the senseless noise of the external world, instead I will bathe in the still waters of my soul.

SEPTEMBER 13 *"Look within, the secret is inside you."*

— Hui-Neng

Meditation: Everything you will ever need along your passage through life exists within the inner recesses of your being. You are supplied with all the resources, maps, blueprints, and vitality that is required to live a peaceful and purposeful life. You must work diligently and navigate according to your higher self in order to fulfill your role here on earth. Outside answers to your questions of existence, happiness, peace, or purpose in your life will forever be out of your reach because they simply do not exist. All the answers reside within you; you may just have to clean up the debris to discover the keys that will unlock your limitless potential.

Ask Yourself: Look deep inside, what is revealed by your soul, how do you plan to manifest these inner visions in your life today?

I Affirm: Today, I will not seek answers outside my being; I will always pose these questions directly to the silent but omnipotent force within.

SEPTEMBER 14 *"Act the part and you will become the part."*

— William James

Meditation: Many people live their entire life dreaming they could do something or become something, but constantly doubt their ability to achieve there inner aspirations. Well here is the cure to this doubt and uncertainty; simply pretend you have the ability to do whatever you desire and act "as if " you are already living this achievement. Visualize yourself accomplishing that which you desire and you will program yourself to achieve this ambition.

Ask Yourself: How will you act "as if " today and pretend that you are well on your way to achievement? You will be amazed at the results of pretending and acting on a daily basis. It is truly amazing; I have tried it and continuously use this brilliant strategy daily. Try it for yourself and I'll see you at the pinnacle of success.

I Affirm: Today, I will play the role that I wish to become.

SEPTEMBER **15**

"Wealth is the ability to fully experience life."

— Henry David Thoreau

Meditation: Take an adventure inside your heart today and discover what you sincerely value in life. I am willing to anticipate that what you truly cherish is not money, power, fortune, or fame. Your heart probably values other important aspects of life such as love, respect, family, true friendship, and your precious children. The true definition of wealth is having an abundance of what you truly value in your life and nothing less. Escape the deluded idea of wealth that haunts the majority and truly assess your wealth based on what your heart and soul treasures.

Ask Yourself: How will you add to your true prosperity today rather than placing significance in external things that actually do not matter much at all?

I Affirm: Today, I will list the 5 things in my life that I genuinely do not want to lose.

SEPTEMBER **16**

"Flow with whatever is happening and let your mind be free. Stay centered by accepting whatever you are doing. This is the ultimate."

— Chuang Tzu

Meditation: Mindfulness in the present moment is the key to absolute tranquility in life. Savor the brilliance and beauty of the single moment right in front of you. This is where you will discover life's true meaning. Live now and become intimate with the moment. Whatever you do in your life today, focus on the feelings it produces, be conscious of each detail of your task, and savor whatever it is you are experiencing right now. Excellence is sure to transpire if you put all your energy, passion, and vitality into each specific task at each specific moment of your life.

Ask Yourself: How will you savor and embrace each moment and experience the eternal NOW?

I Affirm: Today, I will be right where I am, I will cherish exactly what I have, and I will love exactly who I am.

SEPTEMBER 17

"There will always be plateaus in the curve of learning anything. Those who quit at the stagnate times will fail and those that persist will succeed."
— Dale Carnegie

Meditation: At times throughout our life's journey, we will certainly reach places where success seems to be silent and hidden. At these times, be sure not to surrender but to relax and save your energy in order to persist through the hurdles that are placed in front of you. Keep walking the path of spiritual direction and you will prevail. Set yourself apart from those who fail to recognize their dreams and never give up on your inspired pursuit to what you truly deserve.

Ask Yourself: How do you plan not to give up in the silent and motionless times of your excursion through life?

I Affirm: Today, I will sit back and contemplate the success that is unquestionably coming my way.

SEPTEMBER 18

"How can one discover who and what one is without the truth?"
— Nietzsche

Meditation: Everyday, the truth will present itself as an option in your life. You can either choose to reject the truth or accept it and walk along your path in an effort to consistently seek the truth and reality in your life. The truth will open a new world for you and you will be able to live the dreams you were created for. If you choose to walk the path of denial and deception, it will be a prolonged road filled with suffering and frustration. The path of delusion will lead you on a pursuit for pleasure and gratification outside yourself, which will subsequently bring you nothing, but meaninglessness and oblivion in your life. Which path will you travel? We all have the liberty of choosing between the two.

Ask Yourself: What truth about yourself will you allow to enter your life today? Will you rely on truth in life or live in the illusion of the distorted ego?

I Affirm: Today, I will sincerely seek the truth in everything; I will refuse to trust in the explanations of society.

September 19

"If you knew what I know about the power of giving you would not let a single meal pass without sharing it in a single way."

— Buddha

Meditation: Sharing and generosity toward others is the foundation of life and the secret to personal happiness. Human beings were created to give to the world and through the process of giving we receive the precious gifts of serenity and internal exhilaration. Compassionate giving touches our heart and replenishes our energy each day in order to move on consistently and contribute to human kind. To give is an action of unselfish unconditional love for humanity. The person who gives genuinely from his or her heart will be abundantly rewarded.

Ask Yourself: What will you give to the world today without telling anyone?

I Affirm: Today, I will cherish the inherent reward of pure joy that I experience simply by giving of myself to another human being.

September 20

"What you do not want done to yourself, do not do to others."

— Confucious

Meditation: This is the commonsensical solution to all of the world's problems and conflicts. The difficulty remains that the majority of human beings inhabiting this world never gain enough insight and understanding to act upon the tenets of this simple and profound principle. This principle could cure all travesties in the Universe. What we need to do is transcend our egocentric state of being and enter the inner world of our fellow human beings.

Ask Yourself: How will you practice this indispensable principle in your life today?

I Affirm: Today, I will become conscious of the similarity of myself and all other human beings.

SEPTEMBER 21 *"The fruit of love is service which is compassion in action."*
— **Mother Theresa**

Meditation: Of all the things we can do with our life, service to others is the fundamental mission as human beings. There is no other way to enjoy the true meaning and purpose of being alive. There will never be a time when you lend your hand and heart to another human being that you will not feel glorious satisfaction within your heart and soul. This is a basic fact of life. If you merely rush around every day living society's definition of life without realizing the significance of compassion for others, you are unfortunately doomed to a lonely and discontented existence.

Ask Yourself: Whom will you give your heart to freely today?

I Affirm: Today, I will attach compassion and kindness to every action throughout my day.

SEPTEMBER 22 *"We can make a difference in our tomorrows provided we deliver nothing but the very best we can do, everyday."*
— **Og Mandino**

Meditation: Worries about the future often prevent us from performing at our optimal level in the moment today. The simple, but profound secret is that there is no need to worry about the future if you strive for excellence today, because what you do each day adds up to what your future becomes. Get on the path to excellence today and secure what the future holds for you. Be the best human being you can be today and a phenomenal future will be patiently awaiting your arrival.

Ask Yourself: How do you plan on doing your very best today in order to create excellence in your future?

I Affirm: Today. I will put all of my heart and soul into even the smallest tasks.

SEPTEMBER 23

"My philosophy is that not only are you responsible for your life, but doing the best at this moment puts you in the best place for the next moment."

— **Oprah Winfrey**

Meditation: Life is made up of a collection of present moments that provide you with the opportunity to start over and experience a rebirth each day. If we strive for excellence in every moment we are bound to create excellence in our life. Factually speaking, you have control and responsibility for how you and only you act in each moment each day. This is all you have the capacity to control in life. It is up to you personally, what you do right now. If you decide to choose excellence and nothing less in each moment you will create excellence and nothing less in the future of your life.

Ask Yourself: How are you going to strive to do your very best right now at this moment?

I Affirm: Today, I will travel the extra mile throughout my journey, focusing entirely on my behavior and the present moment.

⁌⁍

SEPTEMBER 24

"If you want to be a writer, stop talking about it and sit down and write."

— **Jackie Collins**

Meditation: Many people spend their life sitting around talking about what they want to be, what they want to do, and how life would be much better if they were doing this and that. If you are this type of person you must sit, think, and deeply contemplate what you want to accomplish in life, then make a commitment to begin working on this right now. Working on this is not talking, it is taking the necessary action and following your path of success to the very end.

Ask Yourself: Devise a plan right now to take action toward what you want out of life in order to eliminate the regrets you will feel years from now for not being or doing what burned within you?

I Affirm: Today, I will take the first small step toward accomplishing what I desire in life. My initial step is.

SEPTEMBER 25   *"I like the dreams of the future better than the history of the past."*

— Thomas Jefferson

Meditation: We can all think of many things in the past to feel shameful for, to regret, or to feel guilty about. Let's begin to grow and move on from that useless and unproductive approach to existing and focus on doing our best in this moment in order to evolve and avoid negative feelings about the past. To learn from the past is it's only necessary function and the task of the present is to live and grow and bask in the limitless opportunities that the Universe affords you.

Ask Yourself: What will you do today to create a future that is pleasing to you and to avoid unnecessary regrets throughout the rest of your life?

I Affirm: Today, I will initiate a way of life that does not include dragging the baggage of the past as I proceed along my journey.

—✦═◉═✦—

SEPTEMBER 26   *"In great attempts it is glorious even to fall."*

— Cassius

Meditation: Failure simply enlightens us to the reality that we are growing and taking risks in our lives. It demonstrates to us that we are living innovatively and striving to create adventurous and successful lives. Society teaches us that "failure" is a negative experience; however, society is wrong in this case as well as many others. Welcome and honor "failures" in your life and employ them as instruments for continuous evolution and success on your precious journey.

Ask Yourself: How will you rewire the way that you perceive failure?

I Affirm: Today, I will listen to the language of the Universe when it whispers, "Use this 'failure' as a stepping stone to greatness."

SEPTEMBER **27** *"To err is human, to forgive divine."*

— Alexander Pope

Meditation: Forgiving yourself is the first step in the direction of personal autonomy in your life and forgiving others is the subsequent step necessary to escape the power that is destroying your ability to live a satisfying and peaceful life. Forgiveness will release all the pain embedded in your soul that stops you from genuinely living. Give yourself the precious gift of forgiveness today in order to lighten the load that you carry with you day after day. Alleviate the burden and pain that you put yourself through each and every moment of your existence. You deserve this!

Ask Yourself: What are you not forgiving yourself for in your life? Who have you not forgiven?

I Affirm: Today, I will engage in deep thought and take an honest inventory to discover the hidden resentment that eats at my soul; I will then work on forgiveness to heal the wounds of my being.

SEPTEMBER **28** *"Unhappiness is not knowing what we want and killing ourselves to get it."*

— Don Herold

Meditation: Do you have an idea of what you were brought here to accomplish or are you meaninglessly seeking something outside yourself? Most human beings burden themselves throughout life with the demands of society, the delusions of the ego, and the debris that has developed within their beings. Differentiate yourself from this lot of human beings and discover the true purpose you were born to add to life. Discontinue the endless search for self-gratification and the temporary pleasure of the mind and body. Pursue your worthy meaning in life and contribute positively to the world. This will eliminate unhappiness and produce bliss in your life.

Ask Yourself: What do you truly desire in life and how will you begin creating it now?

I Affirm: Today, I will write my personal and spiritual statement of intent that will act as a guide along my journey.

SEPTEMBER **29** *"The reward of a thing well done is to have done it."*

— **Ralph Waldo Emerson**

Meditation: There are so many astounding accomplishments that we manage to achieve in our lives , however it is odd that we rarely ever give ourselves any recognition or praise for these amazing achievements. Although, we are very hasty to criticize or condemn ourselves for mistakes we believe we have made or experiences in life that we take the blame for. Minimize the negative self-punishing rituals in your life and begin to focus on the outstanding positive accomplishments you manifest in your daily life.

Ask Yourself: How will you begin rewarding yourself for the things you accomplish in your life and forgive yourself for your human behavior?

I Affirm: Today, I will praise myself for the remarkable feats that I accomplish on a daily basis.

SEPTEMBER **30** *"The last of the human freedoms is to choose one's attitudes."*

— **Victor Frankl**

Meditation: It does not matter what the circumstances or situations are in your life, what matters is the attitudes you choose to have in connection with these occurrences. No one can ever seize your ability to create peace, serenity, and happiness in your life. Seek peace and stillness in the chaos of society; this is the secret to a successful and fulfiling life. And, remember never permit the outside world to dictate your thoughts, feelings, beliefs, or attitudes; this is your greatest gift.

Ask Yourself: How will you take control of your inner life today rather than placing it at the dominion of the external world?

I Affirm: Today, I will free myself from the judgments and criticisms of society and bathe in the luminosity and liberation of my inner being.

October

OCTOBER 1

"The big secret in life is that there is no big secret. Whatever your goal, you can get there if you are willing to work."

— Oprah Winfrey

Meditation: Have you ever sincerely sat down and contemplated Your personal goals and desires for your life? Take a few moments and genuinely Reflect on what you want to accomplish in your life. Dig deep and consult your heart on this matter. It is not what society wants for you or what your family wants for you, it is what you truly and deeply desire for you. Life is too precious to allow your dreams and desires to slip away. You deserve this and you have the power to make it happen.

Ask Yourself: Write your goals down today. How can you begin working toward what you deserve in life? Do not waste time; sit down and do it now; this is your valuable life we are talking about.

I Affirm: Today, I will remind myself that I deserve to succeed and enjoy a pleasurable existence.

OCTOBER 2

"It's never too late to be what you might have been."

— George Eliot

Meditation: You are not too old or too tired or too whatever other excuses you plan to give yourself and others. There is no time in your life that it is too late to change your destiny. You are an infinite being and time, to the essence of your being, means nothing. Age means nothing; wrinkles mean nothing, and all the other irrelevant things you obsess over simply mean nothing when considering the reality and truth of your infinite nature. Your soul never ages, it just advances, develops, and evolves to new levels of consciousness.

Ask Yourself: How will you align with the energy of your higher self and work on your childhood dreams of success?

I Affirm: Today, I will not allow any excuses to impede on my journey to the realization of my dreams.

OCTOBER **3** *"For peace of mind, resign as general manager of the Universe."*

— Larry Eisenberg

Meditation: It is very common for human beings to believe that we need to direct the entire world's affairs or at least labor under the illusion that we know exactly how the world should be governed. We often desire to control everything and everyone around us in order to feel manageable in our own life. It is essential to make a commitment to preside over your own world and refrain from attempting to oversee everything else. Peace of mind and contentment come from acceptance of what is and taking care of our personal world.

Ask Yourself: Can you make a commitment to manage your own life today and not buy into the illusion that you have power over anything outside of yourself?

I Affirm: Today, I will discontinue my habitual behavior of trying to control others and concentrate on what I can control, ME.

OCTOBER **4** *"It takes courage to grow up and become who you really are."*

— E. E. Cummings

Meditation: Inside all human beings is a special and unique entity waiting to be born. If we disregard this being and conform to what others want us to be or allow ourselves to be ruled by the tyranny of society we neglect the extraordinary opportunity to know our genuine selves. If we conform and live the illusion of the world we discard the chance to contribute the precious gift of our being to the Universe. It is imperative to engage in the cultivation of our genuine selves and listen attentively to the guidance of our spirit.

Ask Yourself: How can you begin to express the uniqueness of your being today? What are some special and distinctive characteristics of yourself that you conceal most days?

I Affirm: Today, I will take a risk and expose the unique characteristics of my being that I often hide behind my self-created facade.

OCTOBER **5** *"And the trouble is, if you don't risk anything, you risk even more."*

— **Erica Jong**

Meditation: Think about what you desire to achieve in your life, although fear holds you back. Stand up to this fearfulness today and go to battle with the spiritual warrior within. Confronting and fighting through this fear is part of your sacred blueprint and it will allow you to follow the path toward the fulfilment of your higher self. Take action with strength and courage and you will conquer this fear. Do not attempt to obsess or intellectualize your way through the fear; you must take action based on faith and hope and the powerful source that connects you to all things will guide and see you through this obstruction. Fear teaches you to trust in the immense force that lives within you.

Ask Yourself: How will you prevent fear from holding you back from something your heart truly desires? What risk will you take today?

I Affirm: Today, I will begin to recognize that fear's primary purpose is to help me uncover the immense power that lies within my soul.

-+≈-)(≈—+-

OCTOBER **6** When asked what he thought about when he struck out, Babe Ruth said, *"I think about hitting home runs."*
— **Babe Ruth**

Meditation: Life is filled with errors, minor mistakes, failed attempts at goals, and numerous events that we label as "negative." If we focus consistently on these areas of our life and do not appreciate them as learning experiences and opportunities for growth we will not move toward success. The only thing we can actually do with failure is utilize it as a resource for continued determination and persistence. When things appear not to be going your way, continue to visualize success and think positively because this energy will eventually materialize in reality. Do not allow negative and poisonous energy to enter your life when it casually knocks. Negativity is an unwanted and destructive visitor.

Ask Yourself: What will you do to focus on success and positive energy today, no matter what has transpired in your past?

I Affirm: Today, I will not permit negativity to govern my life; I will look for the miracle that is just ahead.

October

OCTOBER **7** *"If we have no peace it is because we have forgotten that we belong together."*
— **Mother Theresa**

Meditation: One of the most healing and profound principles in life is that we human beings are all connected to one another. This is the principle of oneness and this is what rules the entire Universe. Based on this reality, it is very unusual that we continue to exclude human beings based on external characteristics. Do we separate or exclude black dogs from white dogs, purple fish from blue fish, are they different based on their color? We are all part of the same journey we call life and we need each other to succeed and evolve as one race with one purpose.

Ask Yourself: Ponder this principle of unification today and begin bonding with your fellow human beings rather than acting in exclusivity. How will you begin to unite with members of our race, the human race that is?

I Affirm: Today, I will unite with all of humanity and join in the bliss of this intimate connection.

OCTOBER **8** *"Do not take life so seriously, you will never get out of it alive."*
— **Elbert Hubbard**

Meditation: When we depart this earth, we will still have tasks that remain on our "to do" list. Take a break from the chaos of life today and allow the truly important things in your life to matter. It is vital to leave your mind and intellect out of sincerely prioritizing what is important in your life, leave it to your heart and soul, then you will choose what is genuinely precious in your life.

Ask Yourself: Ask your soul what is important today and follow these directions toward reaching out and appreciating the finer things in your life?

I Affirm: Today, I will take the time to be grateful for the priceless things in my life.

OCTOBER **9**

"If you want happiness for an hour—take a nap.
If you want happiness for a day—go fishing.
If you want happiness for a month—get married.
If you want happiness for a year—inherit a fortune.
If you want happiness for a lifetime—help others."
— **Chinese Proverb**

Meditation: You can continue to seek external pleasures or you can choose to experience internal ecstasy. The creation of the life you desire is founded on the basic purpose of all of humanity; this is to connect with every human being and lend your hand and heart whenever another human being is suffering or just needs a friend. Helping others is the way of enlightenment and attainment of genuine success. If you accomplish one thing in your lifetime, it is to lose your self and give your entire being to others.

Ask Yourself: Will you choose temporary and fleeting external pleasures or internal happiness today?

I Affirm: Today, I will contribute a portion of my heart to humanity.

OCTOBER **10**

"You cannot do a kindness too soon, for you never know how soon it will be too late."
— **Ralph Waldo Emerson**

Meditation: To act kind toward another human being is to be kind to yourself. We all expect kindness and we all deserve kindness. Practice kindness throughout your day and be conscious of the feelings it creates within your heart. There are infinite experiences throughout your day to express kindness and compassion toward another living being. It may be simply a smile, a hello, opening a door, or saying thank you. Small acts of kindness have the ability to reform the world. Begin your work as a kind-hearted human being today and the vibrations of kindness will spread rapidly across the vast landscape of the world.

Ask Yourself: What is your plan to be kind to yourself, to others, and to the world today?

I Affirm: Today, I will take advantage of every opportunity to practice an act of kindness.

Your Daily Walk with the Great Minds | 163

OCTOBER **11**

"If you want to make your dream come true the first thing you have to do is wake up."
— **J. M. Power**

Meditation: Well, let's get on with it and begin taking steps to realize your dreams. It is never too late to begin or continue working on aspirations that you have for yourself. Wake up and live your life rather than existing in an imaginary world of stagnation and comfort. Do you want to succeed? Do you want to escape the entrapment of the ordinary? Your creator has nothing less planned for you than the extraordinary, but remember, the Universe affords you a freedom to choose; you can either connect to the flow of limitless and boundless energy or remain chained to the limits and moronic demands of your animalistic ego.

Ask Yourself: How will you begin your progress toward a better future today?

I Affirm: Today, I will awake from my slumber and tap into the limitless potential of my being.

OCTOBER **12**

"One must not hold oneself so divine as to be unwilling occasionally to make improvements in one's creations"
— **Ludwig van Beethoven**

Meditation: Narcissism, which is holding oneself so high and superior to others, but truly feeling horrible about oneself, is the great facade of countless human beings. We hide behind masks, hide from ourselves, but refuse to make changes because we are constantly right about everything. This view and description obviously contradicts itself but this is the great veil we hide behind; one part of ourselves so in love with our perception, our intellect and our creations, but the other part truly loathing ourselves. The solution: Be your true self, continue to advance and make improvements, and never think you are inferior or superior to anyone else in the human race.

Ask Yourself: How will you act as yourself today and be honest with the world? Can you admit that you are not a work of perfection, but a work in progress?

I Affirm: Today, I will work diligently to make improvements in myself.

October

OCTOBER 13

"It is only by forgetting yourself that you draw near to God."

— Henry David Thoreau

Meditation: Self-obsession plagues human's thoughts, beliefs, attitudes, feelings, and, of course, behavior. We always seem to be out for what serves our egoistic needs and will go to any lengths to conquer these selfish wishes. We are always focused on what we need, what we do not have, what we desire, and never thinking about what the totality of creation and humanity needs. It is by detaching from this self-centeredness that we begin to gain awareness into those around us and the presence of the universal architect. Saying good-bye to the ego and its disturbances is the only way that we truly get our spiritual and emotional needs met. Getting out of ourselves and inviting the presence of a higher purpose into our life raises us beyond ordinary consciousness and allows us to bathe in the cascade of divinity.

Ask Yourself: How will you begin to detach from the prison of the selfish ego and enter into the divine presence?

I Affirm: Today, I will enter the spiritual realm of life and leave behind my self-absorbed ego.

OCTOBER 14

"It is my earnest desire to know the will of Providence in this matter. And if I can learn what it is, I will do it."

— Abraham Lincoln

Meditation: Since the divine is omnipresent and connects all things within this Universe, this means we are one with the divine or we are the divine. We have the ability to access the wisdom of Providence and choose to base our decisions on this sacred wisdom or base our decisions on the distorted will of our ego. The choice is always ours, therefore, if we choose to act in connection with the all-pervading source of the creator we will add peace, if we choose the alternative we will add chaos. Which choice will you make?

Ask Yourself: What will you choose to follow today the guidance of your ego or Divine Providence?

I Affirm: Today, I will access the sacred that lies within my soul and use this as a foundation for all my actions.

OCTOBER **15** *"For those who believe, no proof is necessary. For those who don't believe no proof is possible."*
— **John and Lyn St. Clair Thomas**

Meditation: Faith and belief in our higher self always provides us with the truth. The problem is that our ego seeks to separate us from the truth and lives in a world of distortion and denial. Life becomes a constant battle between the delusion of the ego and the truth of our inner being. If we connect to the metaphysical power that creates truth and sincerely trust in this, we will conquer the struggle and walk along side the universal soul; if we fall prey to the ego, we will forever live in the darkness of denial and distortion.

Ask Yourself: What do you fear and lack faith in today? What will you do based on faith and trust today?

I Affirm: Today, I will surrender and allow the Universe to carry me through the day; I will let go of my doubts and trust

⫷⫸

OCTOBER **16** *"Although the world is full of suffering, it is also full of the overcoming of it."*
— **Helen Keller**

Meditation: Pain and suffering is part of the journey of life. It is true that all around us is suffering and anguish, however, who is to say that this is wrong or bad. There is obviously a sophisticated meaning and purpose in it or it would not be an aspect of life. Suffering often teaches us important lessons and allows us to become compassionate helpers of human kind. Without suffering, there would be no joy. Without suffering, there would be no opportunities for human beings to lend compassion and love to others. Of course, suffering causes pain, but it also causes growth and development in the Universe. Maybe we as human beings are not meant to understand the underlying meaning of suffering.

Ask Yourself: How will you contribute the burning compassion that comprises your being?

I Affirm: Today, I will not judge suffering , I will simply accept it take action to relieve it.

OCTOBER **17**

"Many things are lost for want of asking."

— **English Proverb**

Meditation: Do not make assumptions about life. Communicate and ask for what you want and need. There are many problems created by the simple fact that we are fearful of asking others or asking the power beyond us for what we desire. Communicate and discontinue reading the minds of other human beings and the Universe. Asking is a matter of a simple question rather than discarding your needs and moving on without being satisfied. Just ask for what you want, the worst that can happen is the answer will be no.

Ask Yourself: What will you ask another human being for today? What will you ask the omnipotent universal source for today?

I Affirm: Today, I will I ask questions of the Universe and wait quietly for the answers; remember to listen closely because the Universe always responds.

OCTOBER **18**

"We are healed of a suffering, only by experiencing it to the fullest."

— **Marcel Proust**

Meditation: If we stuff our pain and suffering deep down inside of us, it will eventually catch up with us and be released sideways. It is important to express your feelings, emotions, and thoughts on a daily basis to remain clean inside your being. A daily cleansing is worth the benefits of true peace and tranquility. Empty the baggage of the past and stay baggage free from this point on. It is imperative to do a thorough cleaning and then conduct an inventory on a daily basis to free yourself from lugging a bunch of garbage around everywhere you go. If we continue to carry this debris, it will certainly seep out on present experiences. Clean now, so you can have freedom from the bondage of the past.

Ask Yourself: How will you begin to process your pain and suffering from the past? You may want to talk with a therapist, trusting friend, or journal these feelings.

I Affirm: Today, I will begin one of the most vital journeys of my life; I will commence the process of cleaning up the darkness that conceals the radiance of my soul.

October

OCTOBER **19**

"All problems become smaller if you don't dodge them but confront them."
— **William F. Halesy**

Meditation: Avoidance of pertinent issues in your life most often lead to the creation of new difficulties such as frustration, confusion, anxiety, depression, and countless others. Begin to face your challenges head on and this will result in a major reduction of unnecessary chaos in your life and will enhance your much valued self-worth and esteem.

Ask Yourself: What problem will you face head on today without overwhelming fear and debilitating anxiety?

I Affirm: Today, I will use my inner strength and courage to face a difficulty that I have been evading for quite some time now.

OCTOBER **20**

"The measure of your life will not be in what you accumulate but what you give away."
— **Dr. Wayne Dyer**

Meditation: Accumulation of material things throughout our lifetime is very fascinating and tempting to our insatiable ego. Each one of us wants to have it ALL in life. The reality is that the pleasure gained from any of these external sources is merely temporary and will always quickly perish. Then, we move on to the next ego need and on and on with the inexhaustible pursuit of external pleasure. Life is only as pleasurable as we help other human beings to be. If we are not connecting with humanity, we will continue our senseless and unproductive search for transitory pleasures that our ego convinces us to be crucial.

Ask Yourself: Give to somebody today from your heart and compare this with the temporary pleasure of a shot of booze or a new watch. Whom will you give to from your heart today?

I Affirm: Today, I will overcome the temptation of my ego and begin the work of my soul.

OCTOBER 21   *"As long as you're going to think anyway—*
you might as well think BIG."

— Donald Trump

Meditation: We spend every waking and sleeping moment thinking in our lives. Whether you like it or not, you are going to think. Slowly begin transforming your thoughts and beliefs into positive, affirming, and successful thoughts and your life will surely transform. Believe, and all of your desires will be achieved.

Ask Yourself: Can you make a commitment to turn all negative and pessimistic thoughts into positive and affirming thought forms today?

I Affirm: Today, I will notice the thoughts produced by my ego and those produced by my soul; I will make a commitment to nourish only those of the soul.

⊷⊷⧀◉⧁⊶⊶

OCTOBER 22   *"If at first you do succeed try something harder."*

— Ann Landers

Meditation: Do not permit yourself to get comfortable with your knowledge and skills. Push yourself to move forward and evolve in your life. Life is interesting and adventurous if you continue to challenge yourself and take risks. To sit and stagnate in comfort is the way of monotony and boredom. Ultimately, challenging yourself and those around you is the secret to universal growth and evolution.

Ask Yourself: Contemplate and ponder a challenge or adventure that you can embark on today. What is it?

I Affirm: Today, I will give my life the vivacity and passion it deserves.

OCTOBER 23   *"Never undertake anything thinking defeat."*

— Dale Carnegie

Meditation: If you project failure in any situation, you might as well not even attempt to succeed. We create defeat first within our inner self, which then transfers the failure to our external world. Face life each day projecting success with all your internal force, planning for the best outcome, and success will be manifested before your eyes.

Ask Yourself: What will you conquer today in your life?

I Affirm: Today, I will utilize the power of belief in all my endeavors.

OCTOBER 24   *"Wherever you go, go with all your heart."*

— Confucious

Meditation: Opportunities for growth and success are presented to each human being everyday along the path of life. You never know when the correct time or opportunity will come along that will fulfill your purpose in life and lead you toward your dreams. If you are not giving all your heart and soul on a daily basis, you may miss an opportunity of a lifetime. The secret is to give all of your being in everything you do within each and every moment you are alive.

Ask Yourself: How will you vigilantly keep on the look out for opportunities in your life today?

I Affirm: Today, I will live each moment as if it's the final moment of my life; by doing this I will never miss a vital opportunity or build up any regrets.

October

OCTOBER **25**

"There is little sense in attempting to change external conditions, you must first change inner beliefs then outer conditions will change accordingly."
— **Mother Theresa**

Meditation: Our whole life resides in the inner compartments of our being. We must tap into the inner resources and earnestly search and take inventory of our beliefs about the Universe. It does no good to reach outside yourself until the destructive and disillusioned beliefs of the ego are sincerely altered to mirror the truth of the world. All the change that needs to be made in the world has to do with the inner recesses of every human being walking this earth. Once we begin to change the way we perceive life, life will begin to transform in front of our eyes.

Ask Yourself: How will you begin to challenge your beliefs today? What beliefs do you feel are irrational and debilitating in your life?

I Affirm: Today, I will wholeheartedly believe in my innate ability to change my life.

OCTOBER **26**

"People are not lazy. They simply have impotent goals —that is, goals that do not inspire them."
— **Anthony Robbins**

Meditation: We tend to accept and become satisfied with where we are at in our lives. This, of course, is not a problem in itself, however, if you have dreams that you are not striving toward because you have fell into a comfortable rut in life it may be or eventually become an issue. The fact is you have the unlimited ability within this Universe to accomplish anything you believe and work toward. Do you merely want to exist in the comfort of making enough money to cover your bills, to have a monotonous and average job, just to get through each day or do you want and desire greatness and pure bliss. Challenge yourself to achieve excellence and enjoy living a life of a higher and ultimate purpose. The choice remains yours but if you want to achieve extraordinary goals aspire toward them and do not just settle with mediocrity and conformity. It is ultimately up to you; the Universe desires abundance for you if you choose to connect to this force rather than simply live what your ego is satisfied with.

Ask Yourself: What does the higher self within you wish for?

I Affirm: Today I will dare to pursue the what my higher-self yearns for and escape the chains of comfort and mediocrity.

OCTOBER 27

"If you want a quality, act as if you already have it. Try the 'as if' technique."

— William James

Meditation: Figure out who you really want to be, what you really want to do with your life, and what you truly desire and begin to act "as if" these qualities already exist in your life. Act your way into your desired life. The results will certainly amaze you. If you want to run the company your working for, dress the part, act the part, and visualize the part. It may sound rather odd to you but many men and women who have achieved enormous success have productively applied this strategy. Try it, if it does not work for you toss it out. Remember, action is what we are judged by, and from thoughts and beliefs come action. Think, believe, then act according to what and who you aspire to become.

Ask Yourself: What will you act like you have today or what quality will you pretend to have that you truly desire?

I Affirm: Today, I will "act as if" I am well on my way to immense success.

OCTOBER 28

"Creativity can solve almost any problem, the creative act, the defeat of habit by originality, overcomes everything."

— George Lois

Meditation: What habits do you possess that have not been productive or solution centered, but tend to cause more difficulties in your life? Taking new risks and creating original alternatives in your life will lead you into a new dimension of living. Rather than habitually walking along your path in life and doing what unconsciously comes next it is important to seek new solutions, new options, and add creativity to your adventurous passage through this mysterious Universe. Life was meant to be an adventure overflowing with joy and wonder. Explore what is available for you to experience and live a new life of meaning and purpose. Take a step back into the innocence, wonder, and curiosity of your childhood and live this freedom today.

Ask Yourself: How can you utilize creative and alternative solutions today to replace ineffective and unproductive habits?

I Affirm: Today, I will live in a unique and innovative way; I will indulge in the mouth-watering buffet of life.

"To change one's life: Start immediately, do it flamboyantly, no exception, no excuses."
— **William James**

Meditation: There is no better time than right this moment to begin transforming your life. Explore and venture out into the vast ocean of the Universe. There is always room for change and transformation in your life. Revolutionize your current way of living and marvel in the wonders of this exceptional opportunity to change right now. Make a decision to abandon your old way of thinking, believing, and living and renovate your inner self. All of this is possible and starts from making a firm decision right now and following the guidance of the spectacular force, which awaits your companionship.

Ask Yourself: What do you desire to change in your life and how will you begin it right NOW?

I Affirm: Today, I will unconditionally trust in my capacity to change anything I am determined and passionate about changing in my life.

"Strong lives are motivated by dynamic purposes."

— **Kenneth Hildebrand**

Meditation: Do you know what your essential purpose is in life? Your purpose is what will guide you along your journey of life and lead you to physical, mental, and spiritual prosperity. This purpose is why you are here and what you can uniquely add to the Universe in order to take part in the evolution of the world's consciousness. You are an important element in humanity's expansion and development.

Ask Yourself: Are you living according to an extraordinary and energizing purpose today or do you need to ponder what your purpose consists of? Hint: Ego-related purposes, such as hoarding financial accomplishments, having the best stuff on the block, or collecting brand name items will not take you on this incredibly enlightening path of the spirit.

I Affirm: Today, I will devote myself to the internal purpose that burns within my soul.

OCTOBER 31

"Creative minds always have been known to survive any kind of bad training."
— **Anna Freud**

Meditation: Life is an enlightening and enjoyable journey of learning and relearning. It is always harmful to believe everything you were taught or what you read; it is necessary to explore and examine knowledge in order to search and discover the truth. It is imperative that you search within your heart and question your past teachings, especially if they do not truly make sense to you. The Universe always has the truth; listen carefully and it will be revealed to you.

Ask Yourself: What will you question today to further search and discover the truth?

I Affirm: Today, I will contemplate my past education and question anything that does not align with my true beliefs.

NOVEMBER 1 *"To the dull mind all of nature is leaden. To the illuminated mind the whole world sparkles with light."*

— **Ralph Waldo Emerson**

Meditation: The Universe gives us a choice with regard to how we choose to experience the world. We can be delighted and amazed by the phenomena that surrounds us and be mindful of the precious gifts that the Universe provides us with or, on the other hand, we can walk the earth ignoring all the beauty that it offers. The true beauty and amazement in life originates within your spirit, whether you choose to connect your life to this source or merely walk alone with your ego is probably the most influential decision you will ever make.

Ask Yourself: How will you open your eyes and heart to the immense beauty of life today?

I Affirm: Today, I will awake from the ignorance of my ego and enjoy the mystery of the Universe.

NOVEMBER 2 *"Don't compromise yourself, you are all you got."*

— **Janis Joplin**

Meditation: We are all unique and exceptional individuals with our heart felt dreams, ideals, beliefs, values, and desires. Life is a continuous process of discovering ourselves and loving who we truly are. Do not ever compromise who you truly are within and never question your worth no matter what others say or do around you. You are the only you in this Universe and you have a special purpose and significance for being here. Explore the feelings of your heart, let them emanate from your being and express your distinctive vibrancy every precious moment of your existence. Be free and take pleasure in being you.

Ask Yourself: How will you express your genuine self today without compromising your integrity and worth as a unique individual?

I Affirm: Today, I will step out from behind my mask and express the incredible being that I am.

November

NOVEMBER 3 *"You, as much as anybody in the entire Universe, deserve your love and affection."*

— Buddha

Meditation: Throughout our lives, we often spend a majority of our time thinking and doing for others. It is vital that you take care of yourself, love yourself, and realize the uniqueness and magnitude of who you are. You must take care of you before you can take care of anyone else. You are the most important person in your life and it is vital to internalize and live this central principle in your passage through life.

Ask Yourself: How will you care for yourself today and express compassionate and unconditional self-love?

I Affirm: Today, I will be the recipient of the immense love that resides within my heart.

NOVEMBER 4 *"Cherish your visions and your dreams as they are the children of your soul; the blue prints of your ultimate achievements."*

— Napoleon Hill

Meditation: Give up your monotonous, average, so called "normal" routine today and take some risks in your life. Create an adventurous existence. Begin living your dreams and begin manifesting what it is you desire to leave for the next generation. Start right this moment. Visualize and fanaticize what you would like your life to look like and begin creating this masterpiece NOW.

Ask Yourself: What small step will you take today to begin living your dreams and make use of your innate potential to succeed?

I Affirm: Today, I will begin living the life that often penetrates my daydreams.

NOVEMBER **5** *"People are lonely because they build walls instead of bridges."*

— Joseph F. Newton

Meditation: It has unfortunately become rather widespread for human beings to hide or disappear behind sophisticated facades and close themselves off to the rest of the Universe. They create their self-made comfortable world that is devoid of growth and success. This world has no possibility of becoming a better place until we begin to open ourselves up to others and get to know the rest of our race. Take off your mask and express your humanity among all members of the Universe; it may be frightening at first, but in the end, it will benefit you and the world and will open up new opportunities in your life.

Ask Yourself: How will you put your self-made wall down just for today and embrace your connection to humanity?

I Affirm: Today, I will express my genuine self with all of its unique and distinguishing qualities; I will not suppress the real ME.

NOVEMBER **6** *"I couldn't wait for success so I went ahead without it."*

— Jonathan Winters

Meditation: Many individuals sit around and wait for their so-called time in the spotlight, their great break at last, and the fortune that they feel they deserve in life. If you continue using this strategy you may be waiting a very long time. Stand up and take responsibility for creating and discovering the success you deserve in life. It all comes from personal responsibility and taking action toward your goals and desires. If you linger around you may be giving up your opportunity for success. Find your personally defined success and run with it with all the determination and passion the Universe has granted you.

Ask Yourself: How will you take responsibility and the necessary action to discover your personal success today?

I Affirm: Today, I will contemplate what success means to me and keep this definition always by my side.

NOVEMBER 7 *"Every time you don't follow your inner guidance, you feel a loss of energy, loss of power, and a sense of spiritual deadness."*

— Shakti Gawain

Meditation: Stop allowing life to drain you of internal energy and get back on your destined spiritual path. Follow the inner brilliance that you were born with and revitalize your spirit today. This loss of energy and spiritual lethargy is created when we take our personal ego-based will back and disconnect from the universal link that provides eternal guidance and truth in our lives. Getting off the path to enlightenment and taking the whole world in your hands always results in loss of energy and vitality. The important thing to know is that it is a choice that you have the freedom to make. If you have taken a diversion from your energizing path, make a personal decision to get back on and utilize the omnipotent source that provides you with everything you need.

Ask Yourself: What do you need to do to discontinue the energy draining activities in your life and get back on your innate spiritual route to success?

I Affirm: Today, I will ask the Universe to gently nudge me back on the path to illumination.

NOVEMBER 8 *"Angels fly because they take themselves lightly."*

— G. K. Charleston

Meditation: Discontinue taking yourself so seriously. Life is a dress rehearsal for eternity and you are performing just fine. You are human and were created and expected to make mistakes in life in order to spiritually evolve. Laugh at yourself today and take a break from the chaos and pettiness of daily societal life. Sit back, relax, and have fun in some special way. Play, jump around, giggle, and let your innocent and blissful child escape the boundaries of the rigidity and seriousness of your ego.

Ask Yourself: What can you say to yourself or do when you recognize that you are taking your self and life too damn serious?

I Affirm: Today, I will rescue the soul of my inner child and enjoy the ecstasy-filled Universe.

NOVEMBER 9 *"The world is my country, all mankind my brethren, and to do good is my religion."*

— Thomas Paine

Meditation: Exclusive human institutions are pervasive throughout this world. In reality there is only one race that we belong to, the human race. We are all connected and it is necessary to realize this, believe this, and begin applying this principle in order for the world to evolve beyond the current stagnation. Stop excluding human beings just like yourself. Differences in race, nationality, religion, and all the other rationales for excluding others are unique characteristics that need to be honored and embraced. This diversity is the quintessence of the Universe. Enter the oneness that exists in the Universe, lend a hand to your fellow human beings, and know and love them as equals.

Ask Yourself: How will you connect to the one and only race today and discontinue the exclusivity in your life?

I Affirm: Today, I will strive to eliminate the idiocy of exclusiveness in my life; I will begin reaching higher than my ego and contribute to the evolution of the humanity.

NOVEMBER 10 *"There are no mistakes, no coincidences. All events are blessings given to us to learn from."*
— Elizabeth Kubler-Ross

Meditation: Life is a complex puzzle that will forever remain a work in progress. Each day different pieces are presented to us by the Universe. It is our responsibility to place them in the proper place in order to advance along our journey. It is vital that you are mindful of the pieces that are revealed to you. Creatively and intelligently arranging these puzzle pieces will make all the difference.

Ask Yourself: How will you be mindful of each piece of the Universal puzzle today?

I Affirm: Today, I will efficiently use and take advantage of all the blessings that the Universe graciously bestows upon me.

NOVEMBER 11 *"Surrender doesn't obstruct our power it enhances it."*

— Marianne Williamson

Meditation: Growing up in this world, we are often taught to never surrender. Surrender is labeled as a weak, negative, and disempowering activity. This perception is incorrect and needs to be reframed within our storehouse of knowledge. Surrendering to life's problems and difficulties and allowing the Universe to be our partner is the correct strategy. This will ultimately lead to success and spiritual peace. Surrender allows for the wisdom and divine intelligence of the world to work on your difficulties and come to an innovative solution.

Ask Yourself: How will you surrender in order to gain control of your life today?

I Affirm: Today, I will capitalize on this enlightening paradox—"Surrender to Win."

NOVEMBER 12 *"Though no one can go back and make a brand new start, anyone can start from now and make a brand new ending."*

— Unknown Author

Meditation: Each day brings an entirely new lifetime to live. This life only lasts twenty-four hours and asks you to provide the best performance possible for this time period. Begin in this twenty-four-hour period to live according to your dreams and desires and commence living the life you were meant to live. It is never too late to change your direction in life and achieve what you imagined as an innocent child with idealism and wonder.

Ask Yourself: What do you want to be remembered for in this lifetime? What do you desire to leave the Universe when you transcend this part of your journey?

I Affirm: Today, I will transcend the illusion of time and live fully in this present moment.

NOVEMBER 13

"The best way out of a problem is through it."

— Unknown Author

Meditation: We often attempt to maximize pleasure and minimize pain; this is the human condition. When a challenge or difficulty arises in our life we would much rather run, escape, avoid, or tip-toe around the problem. Although, by doing this, we often prolong the difficulty and the pain and prohibit our learning. The Universe presents you with these situations in order to learn and grow, thus, we must complete this process or this challenge will continue to repeat itself. The Universe knows exactly what it is doing when it sets an obstacle in your way. It is your role to conquer and evolve from the unique learning experience.

Ask Yourself: How will you confront your problems head on today and move directly through them rather than procrastinating and regressing?

I Affirm: Today, I will take action immediately when a "problem" arises; there is no sense it dragging it along.

NOVEMBER 14

"If you want others to be happy, practice compassion. If you want to be happy practice compassion."
— H. H. The Dalai Lama

Meditation: Compassion very simply is the key to healing and serenity. We must first have compassion for ourselves and then transform that compassionate energy to others. All healing and human growth is based on a foundation consisting of compassion and love. These two qualities have the capacity to revolutionize the way humanity lives in this Universe. If we practice these qualities, we will surly help ourselves, but most importantly, the vibrational energy connected to our compassion will positively affect the vast Universe that surrounds us.

Ask Yourself: How will you practice compassion for yourself and others throughout your journey today?

I Affirm: Today, I will enrich humanity by practicing compassion and kindness in all my actions.

NOVEMBER 15

"We are all authors of our years, and our failures and defeats are only steps to something better."
— Og Mandino

Meditation: If we did not have the struggles and challenges in our life, we would never be urged to grow and improve. Everything good in life is created from a series of failures and defeats. Allow yourself to learn from each failure and continue to strive for your personalized fairy tale. Invent your novel of success and continue to work through the obstacles of learning that your creator puts in front of you. All complications and challenges are meant to take place exactly where and when they occur and your role is to unscramble the puzzle that is presented and continue with the universal purpose you were brought here to accomplish.

Ask Yourself: What do you plan to do when faced with a challenge or difficulty in your life today?

I Affirm: Today, I will not attempt to avoid difficulties but I will welcome them as sacred signs directing me toward excellence.

⊷⟶◉⟵⊶

NOVEMBER 16

"Don't think you are on the right road just because it's a well beaten path."
— Unknown author

Meditation: True brilliance is defined by the creation of more spiritual and fulfiling paths that have never been trampled upon. Genuine success is achieved by thrusting ahead and making your own passageway for the world to eventually follow. Be a leader and create an innovative corridor that will lead to the transformation of the Universe. Prevent yourself from following the path of the majority opinion, the path of least resistance, the path of society, or any other path founded on misconception and delusion. Create your personal and spiritual path founded on the eternal virtues of truth, honesty, and commitment to a higher and worthwhile purpose.

Ask Yourself: Would you like to conform and do what everyone else is carelessly doing or do you desire to express your true inner genius? How do you plan to make this unique expression a part of the world?

I Affirm: Today, I will take the road less traveled.

NOVEMBER 17

"You have enemies? Good, that means you stood up for something sometime in your life."
— **Winston Churchill**

Meditation: In this world, courage, strength, and genius are often met with great opposition from other human beings who applying these qualities in their lives. Accept these individuals, treat them kindly and move on with your enlightened journey. These people are just there to test your perseverance and teach you vital lessons in living. These enemies are actually the greatest teachers you will ever encounter.

Ask Yourself: What can you learn today from your so-called "enemies" that have been placed in your path?

I Affirm: Today, I will have compassion for those that have attempted to hurt me and most importantly, I will internalized the profound lessons they have taught me.

NOVEMBER 18

"The pessimist sees the difficulty in every opportunity; the optimist, the opportunity in every difficulty."
— **L. P. Jacks**

Meditation: Life is an incredible journey that presents us with many clues throughout our voyage. In order to seize these opportunities to success, we must be in tune with the spirit of the Universe and be open and willing to internalize and utilize these gifts. Remain focused on your desired path to success and walk courageously through all difficulties in your way. You will come out on the other side transformed and stronger after each challenge and difficulty is conquered.

Ask Yourself: How can you begin to look at each moment of your life today as a clue to success and take the time to see where these clues will lead you?

I Affirm: Today, I will not overlook any clue that the Universe places in my path.

NOVEMBER **19**

"In every real man a child is hidden that wants to play."

— Nietzsche

Meditation: Spirituality in its genuine form is going back to experiencing and becoming that innocent child that you once were. To be non-judgmental, enthusiastic about life, and amazed by the simple yet profound aspects of each new experience. To allow yourself to become a child again is to truly become alive. Let your inner child out to play and find joy in the many wonders of the Universe. To go back to this state of bliss, innocence, and freedom is to experience the essence of spirituality.

Ask Yourself: How will you release your inner child from the private chambers of your serious adult being?

I Affirm: Today, I will allow the child within me to experience the wonder and ecstasy found in each moment.

NOVEMBER **20**

"Conformity is the jailer of freedom and the enemy of growth."

— John F. Kennedy

Meditation: Break out of the prison of your mind and escape from the confinement created by society. Leap into the boundless energy of the spirit and allow your inner self to grow beyond your imagination. There are no walls, cells, or boundaries that stunt or imprison our growth unless we create them ourselves or allow society to dictate our experience in life. Embrace your individual freedom and the unlimited potential for growth in your life. Express your internal creativity and imagination and your life will advance beyond your dreams.

Ask Yourself: How will you open your mind to endless possibilities today and give it the power to imagine and believe that anything is possible?

I Affirm: Today, I will abandon the negativity and doubt of the ego and unite with the boundless energy of the Universe.

NOVEMBER 21

"When the world says 'give up'
Hope whispers, 'try it one more time'."
— **Unknown Author**

Meditation: Hope is what carries you through each day continuously letting you know that better days and bigger accomplishments are right around the corner. Cherish your daily experience in life and hold on tight to hope. With hope, you are bound to succeed in whatever you long for in your life. Live with infinite hope and undying faith and you will truly experience peace and tranquility.

Ask Yourself: In what area of your life will you stop listening to the world and tune into the silent whisper of hope?

I Affirm: Today, when the world exclaims "GIVE UP", I will respond with a gentle whisper , "I have found HOPE".

NOVEMBER 22

"People who do not experience self-love have little or
no capacity to love others."
— **Nathanial Branden**

Meditation: Remember, you are your best friend, lover, and inspiration above all others. Give yourself what you need, what you desire, and most importantly give yourself love on a daily basis. Uncover the priceless jewel that resides within your being and continue to polish this treasure on a daily basis. You deserve the love you provide for yourself and by loving your entire being you will gain the unlimited capacity to share your love and kindness with everyone who crosses your path.

Ask Yourself: How will you demonstrate your love for yourself today?

I Affirm: Today, I will give myself the nourishment and love that I genuinely deserve.

NOVEMBER 23

"True thanksgiving means that we need to thank God for what he has done for us , and not to tell him what we have done for him."
— **George R. Hendrick**

Meditation: It is truly amazing how much the universal force does for us on a daily basis. It guides us toward peace and happiness every moment of our existence and asks for nothing in return. This force is selfless, loving, and non-judgmental. The source provides us with unconditional love and compassion. It also allows us to choose to be connected to the Universe or to follow the guidance of our self will. All of this without any expectations for reimbursement. Without this force, we are nothing; when connected and linked to this force, we are everything. The least you can do today is express your gratitude and detach from your ego's need to take credit for all of your accomplishments.

Ask Yourself: Who and what are you thankful for today?

I Affirm: Today, I will tell those in my life as well as my higher power how much I appreciate them.

⋄⇥⟞⟝⇤⋄

NOVEMBER 24

"Learn to get in touch with the silence within yourself and know that everything in life has a purpose."
— **Elizabeth Kubler-Ross**

Meditation: There is absolutely nothing that happens along your journey in life that is not part of the precise Universal Design. Your soul continues to unfold and fulfill its ultimate task through every moment you are alive. Observe and embrace the whole of life and enjoy each moment you are given as a gift of life. Connect to the harmony of the Universe and you will be lead to the higher dimensions of consciousness where you will see truth and purpose surrounding your being. Live passionately and pursue your sacred purpose, this is truly what life is all about.

Ask Yourself: What will you do today to awaken yourself to the purpose that lies within everything and every moment of life?

I Affirm: Today, I will not allow anyone or anything to stand in my way along my path to a higher purpose.

NOVEMBER 25 *"The less you open your heart to others the more your heart suffers."*
— **Deepak Chopra**

Meditation: Your heart's supreme purpose is to love passionately with infinite compassion and kindness. When we keep this love from others, we cause suffering and wounds to our own heart. Release the intense love and kindness that burns within you to all you encounter today. This is the true meaning of life and love is what powers this Miraculous Universe. There is no force that compares to the potency and vigor of love.

Ask Yourself: Who will you offer your heart to today and share your precious and powerful gift of love?

I Affirm: Today, I will live my life with unconditional love for all of humanity.

⤛⟿◉⟿⤜

NOVEMBER 26 *"How wonderful it is that nobody need wait a single moment before starting to improve the world."*
— **Anne Frank**

Meditation: Improving the world is a spiritual responsibility for every human being that inhabits the Universe. If we are not improving the world around us, than what are we doing? The answer is either being stagnate or being destructive. Improvement of the world begins with one human being and blossoms across all of humanity. Advancement in humanity begins with the beliefs and dreams of one human being, which then transpires through united action among communities, societies, and eventually all cultures.

Ask Yourself: Can you incorporate making an improvement in the world into your "To Do" list today? What priority will this task get?

I Affirm: Today, I will live by this motto: " I have but one goal in my life and that is to transform the world."

NOVEMBER 27

"Life is raw material. We are artisan. We can sculpt our existence into something beautiful, or debase it into ugliness."
— Cathy Bettis

Meditation: Immerse yourself into the eternal glow of the spirit and create the beauty that is overflowing from your heart and soul. Life is your personal masterpiece, which awaits your artistry. Utilize your personal and spiritual talent to illustrate the life that you envision for you and all of humanity. With diligence and persistence, you can begin materializing this vision in reality. What you desire is at your fingertips and you have all the power to manifest it if you have the passion and determination to see it to fruition.

Ask Yourself: How will you create the image that lies inside your heart waiting to be born?

I Affirm: Today, I will embark on the creation of the masterpiece of my life.

NOVEMBER 28

"To do a common thing uncommonly well brings success."
— Henry John Heinz

Meditation: No matter what your life's work is, if you perform it with love, passion, and determination, you are guaranteed success. Break out of merely doing your job to get by and seize the miraculous opportunity of greatness that awaits you.. You were programmed to become an enormous influence to the world around you. You have miracles embedded into your soul awaiting manifestation. Awaken the electricity that flows through your inner being and materialize success in all aspects of your life.

Ask Yourself: What will you do with passion today that you ordinarily perform just to get by and receive a paycheck?

I Affirm: Today, I will put my complete being in my ordinary daily activities.

NOVEMBER 29 *"No culture can live if it attempts to be exclusive."*

— M. K. Gandhi

Meditation: Currently, the state of the Universe is depressing and full of suffering due to the presence of one destructive force. This force is exclusivity; that is our idea of being separate based on outside characteristics and excluding valuable human beings based on these physical and ego driven traits. This is pathetic and pure insanity. The only principle that can save us from the devastating effects of this is love. This means a demonstration of love for the totality of humanity and embracing the unity and oneness of all living beings.

Ask Yourself: How will you begin expressing love for humanity today and embrace the reality and truth of unity and oneness in the Universe?

I Affirm: Today, I will unite with the whole of humanity, rather than feeding into my ego's need to be separate.

NOVEMBER 30 *"Man cannot discover new oceans until he has courage to lose sight of the shore."*

— Unknown Author

Meditation: It is vital that you remain conscious of and continuously believe that everything is possible and you must not allow others to negate your thoughts, beliefs, dreams, or ideas. This Universe is yours to discover and you have the capacity to create anything you truly desire in your life. You simply need to confront your fears, take risks, and proceed with passion and determination. Your higher-self has no limits and has no fears, however it is necessary to detach from your ego in order to access the higher being that resides within you.

Ask Yourself: How will you begin your voyage into your inner most dreams and desires?

I Affirm: Today, I will take a risk that I have been holding back from for much to long.

DECEMBER 1 *"Life is either a daring adventure or nothing."*

— **Helen Keller**

Meditation: Make your life nothing less than a magnificent adventure. You were not created unique and brilliant to live in the comfort and monotony of societal life. You are here to make a substantial effect on the state of the world today and with this responsibility come risks, danger, obstacles, and never-ending adventure. Society and others around you attempt to silence this reality; however, you must battle these forces and continue traveling your purpose-filled mission. You are a Warrior with your spirit as your ally. Begin your arduous but rewarding journey right now and the Universe will compensate you with abundance and everlasting contentment.

Ask Yourself: What will you plan to do or take action on today that will be daring and adventurous?

I Affirm: Today, I will fill my life with risk and adventure.

DECEMBER 2 *"We can know God easily as long as we do not find it necessary to define him."*

— **Basil King**

Meditation: The omnipotent energy of the Universe is beyond our intellectual understanding and human terminology. We cannot possibly put this Supreme Power into any words or categories created by human beings. We must feel this power with all of our being and attach to it internally. To know this source is to know love.

Ask Yourself: How will you accept not understanding, but relying on faith and trust pertaining to the creative energy today?

I Affirm: Today, I will stop trying to discover my spirituality by intellectually analyzing it.

December

DECEMBER 3 *"Man is only miserable so far as he thinks himself so."*

— Jacopo Sannazaro

Meditation: Take control of your destiny starting right now. Do not allow the influence of situations, people, or any external event to dictate how you think, feel, or act. You are completely in control of the path you take in life. The question is, do you want to take responsibility for this great task? Of course, you can project the blame of your misery, failure, despair, and defeat on the outside world, but this is sheer denial and self-delusion. Prepare yourself to be happy, content, and satisfied with your life and this will be what you experience. It is your great ability, how you use it is certainly your decision.

Ask Yourself: How will you take responsibility for your being today rather than allowing external things to dictate your destiny?

I Affirm: Today, I will take responsibility for thought, beliefs, attitudes, and behaviors; this is truly all I have control of in life.

DECEMBER 4 *"If we could read the secret history of our enemies, we would find in each mans life a sorrow and a suffering enough to disarm all hostility."*

— Henry Wadsworth Longfellow

Meditation: Today, attempt to feel empathy and enter the inner world of those that you feel anger toward. It is imperative to keep in mind that we are all human beings trying to survive our journey of life and we all have struggles and pain from the past. Suffering is universal and is only relieved by compassion and understanding of other human beings. What do you need when you suffer? Whatever you answer is what you should provide to other suffering beings.

Ask Yourself: Who will you feel empathic for and treat with compassion in your life today?

I Affirm: Today, I will practice empathy in my relationships with other human beings.

December

DECEMBER 5 *"Live in the present as much as possible, past and future a merely thoughts, the present is life."*
— **Dr. Richard Carlson**

Meditation: Our minds are sophisticated tools for life, although, when we live completely in our heads rather than living in life, we are unfortunately and unproductively misusing our thinking faculties. The present is all that exists, all that is real, and it is all that can be changed. Many lives have been destroyed by the illusory thoughts of the past and future. From now on, do not waste any more precious time, energy, or emotion on these delusions. Bask in the illumination and the bliss of the present and discover the magic and the power of NOW.

Ask Yourself: How will you focus all of your energy on the present moment today?

I Affirm: Today, I will simply BE.

DECEMBER 6 *"Never, never, never, never, never, never, never, never, never, never, never give up!"*
— **Winston Churchill**

Meditation: I hope that this expresses clearly the persistence and perseverance that you need to practice in your life. No matter what goes on in your life, never give up on your path to success, yourself, or your personal and spiritual growth. All worthy things in life are achieved by determination and seeing your goal to the very end. Get on your path and stay on your path until you are satisfied with your results. If there is one trait that all great achievers have in common, it is surely passionate determination and persistence toward what they desire in their lives and the life of the Universe.

Ask Yourself: How will you be persistent in all your goals and desires today and not resign no matter what is placed in your path?

I Affirm: Today, I will keep in mind that it is not acceptable to give up prior to reaching my ultimate desires; If I want something I can have it as long as I put in the labor required.

DECEMBER **7** *"To think too long about doing a thing often becomes its undoing."*

— **Eva Young**

Meditation: Human beings are thinking animals and we often spend a majority of our time between our ears obsessing profusely. However, life is also about doing and being. If we are trapped in the little circus in our heads for too long, we begin to lose consciousness of the outside world called life. This constant obsessing and intellectualizing will drain you of life energy and keep you from enthusiastically living the life that your inner self desires. Do not get enthralled by the egos intellectual demands and delusions. Step out of your cerebral playground and enjoy the wonders of the external Universe and all its precious jewels.

Ask Yourself: How can you limit your thoughts today and begin doing, acting, being, and experiencing life to its fullest beyond your logical mind?

I Affirm: Today, I will prevent my mind from hindering my enjoyment in the activity of just being.

DECEMBER **8** *"All miseries derive from not being able to sit quietly in a room alone."*

— **Blaise Pascal**

Meditation: Solitude is an extremely important aspect of your life. It is necessary to get to know and appreciate yourself in order to connect in a healthy and advantageous manner to other human beings. Take a few minutes alone and focus specifically on you. Focus on your breath, your feelings, your thoughts, and try to become acquainted with yourself a little each day. Begin to harness the energy within you and see yourself as a special and unique human being that is extremely vital to the growth and advancement of humankind. Within the depths of your being resides a priceless gem that needs to be discovered, polished, and expressed in your daily life.

Ask Yourself: When will you take time to spend with yourself today? Where will you do this?

I Affirm: Today, I will embrace and honor what I discover on my inner voyage and make a commitment to further the development of my genuine self.

DECEMBER **9** "Munich School Master evaluation of Ten Year Old Albert Einstein: *"You'll never amount to much."*
— Munich School Master

Meditation: Here is one crucial reason that you cannot allow others to have influence over who you are and what you become in life. You and every individual that walks this earth has their special inner genius; if we search and seek with determination, honesty, and passion, this treasure will be discovered and expressed in your life. You can be phenomenal, extraordinary, unique, special, and anything else you desire as long as you put your energy into discovering this within you and collaborating with the Universe in order to reveal this in your reality.

Ask Yourself: How will you innovatively create your life today rather than allowing others to dictate what you do and become?

I Affirm: Today, I will hold the power and influence regarding what I do and become in my life.

DECEMBER **10** *"I want to know Gods thoughts; the rest are details."*
— Albert Einstein

Meditation: It is quite satisfying and enlightening to know that a brilliant man of science such as Albert himself prioritized his life. What does your creator want from you, and what were you created specifically to accomplish in this Universe; these are the main existential questions that you need to contemplate on a daily basis. To be of use and purpose to the universal condition is the greatest of life's gifts. A purpose and meaning in life is what will get you through anything the world hands you.

Ask Yourself: How will you do what you were created to do today and what is your plan to continue doing this in your daily existence?

I Affirm: Today, I will listen to the Mind of the Universe.

DECEMBER 11

"Take a chance. All life is a chance. The man who goes furthest is generally the one willing to do and dare."

— Dale Carnegie

Meditation: Venture out and manifest the potential that lies within your unique spirit. Penetrate the boundaries of society and your ego and follow the inner guidance of your soul. You certainly have the ability to choose to follow your ego or be lead by the higher consciousness within you. Your higher self craves and yearns for adventure and taking risks associated with life. Take a chance today and embark on an activity that lies outside the self-imposed boundaries that your ego restricts you to.

Ask Yourself: Will you choose to be controlled by your ego today or follow the divine guidance that lies within you?

I Affirm: Today, I will nourish the part of me that seeks adventure and risk; I will remember that nothing great has ever been accomplished without taking risks.

DECEMBER 12

"Here is the test to find out whether your mission on earth is finished: If you're alive it isn't."

— Richard Bach

Meditation: You are still here on earth because you have not completed the work you were created to accomplish. Get to it, begin accessing the limitless potential within you, and pursue your ultimate ambition with enthusiasm and resolve. You will remain here until your job is completed, so enjoy your daily journey and make the best of each moment you are blessed with this precious gift of life.

Ask Yourself: How will you continue your mission on earth and fulfill your soul's responsibility here?

I Affirm: Today, I will continue my soul's work with vigor and passion.

DECEMBER 13   *"To improve is to change, to be perfect is to change often."*
— Winston Churchill

Meditation: Change is inevitable in life and it is imperative that we always remain open-minded and eager to change and cultivate our being in every instant of our daily lives. If we do not change, nothing in our life changes. Changing and nurturing the treasured aspects that lie deep within our beings is a vital component of healthy and successful living. To be rigid and inflexible is to die an early death and resist transforming as the Universe advances along its evolution.

Ask Yourself: How will you apply open-mindedness and willingness in order to grow and change today?

I Affirm: Today, I will participate in the evolution of the Universe by engaging in Transformative Living; that is to say I will seek change in every moment of my life.

DECEMBER 14   *"Perseverance is the hard work you do after you get tired of doing the hard work you already did."*
— Newt Gingrich

Meditation: When you are feeling the lethargy of the day, this is a sign that your ego has completed what it will be able to accomplish and has gone as far as it is willing to go. The ego is very satisfied at this point to give up, pack it in, call it a day, and hit the couch to watch television. The spirits work is composed of what we call perseverance; this is when you have gone beyond the physical and mental pain of the ego and continued pushing toward success. This is when all the inner resources of your soul are called upon to go above and beyond the mediocrity of the physical self. This is the time when greatness and works of genius are created.

Ask Yourself: Will you allow your spirit to go the extra mile today?

I Affirm: Today, I will transcend the ego and tap into the exceptional ability of my eternal spirit.

DECEMBER **15**

"A man sooner or later discovers that he is the master gardener of his soul, the director of his life."

— James Allen

Meditation: Throughout our life, we make a variety of discoveries and gain an abundance of knowledge concerning all arenas of life. If you have not learned yet or still doubt in your mind that you create the life you live, please internalize and begin to believe it now so you can begin constructing the unique creation of your existence. Take action today and visualize what you long for in your life and set out to make it become a reality.

Ask Yourself: How will you begin to invent the life you hunger for today?

I Affirm: Today, I will nourish my precious soul and allow it to evolve without the impediment of societal delusions.

⋆⇥━●━●━⇤⋆

DECEMBER **16**

"Difficulties strengthen the mind as labor does the body."

— Seneca

Meditation: As you probably have noticed more than once, life is arduous at times. You must accept this and move through the difficult times in order to build and strengthen your mental endurance. The more we endure the more satisfying and peaceful our lives will become. The harder the times you experience the greater rewards are to come. Difficulty always lies in the path toward outstanding achievements.

Ask Yourself: How do you plan to exercise your mind today?

I Affirm: Today, I will utilize my creative inheritance perceive difficulties in a positive manner.

DECEMBER **17**

"If we are to live together in peace we must come to know each other better."
— **Lyndon Johnson**

Meditation: Exclusiveness is one of the most destructive elements presently causing devastation to societies, cultures, religions, races, and all other institutions throughout the world. If we are to prosper as a race, we must begin to internalize the realization that there is only one race, the human race. Experiencing and savoring the vast diversity that the world offers is a precious gift for each human being in this Universe. We are not using it or honoring this as a gift but we are using it as a nuclear weapon that threatens to destroy humanity and the entire cosmos. Exclusivity and segregation based on petty outside difference kills more human beings and ruins more human lives than anything throughout the history of humankind.

Ask Yourself: How will you be inclusive throughout your day today and pay tribute to the diversity of humanity?

I Affirm: Today, I will savor the incredible beauty that the diversity of the Universe offers me.

⟡

DECEMBER **18**

"Formulate and stamp indelibly on your mind a mental picture of yourself as succeeding. Hold this picture tenaciously. Never permit it to fade. Your mind will seek to develop the picture...Do not build up obstacles in your imagination."
— **Norman Vincent Peale**

Meditation: Whatever you truly believe deep within your being and visualize clearly within your soul you will certainly accomplish. Never allow negativity to impact your vision and always believe in yourself. This picture of success that you conceive will begin to transpire one moment at a time if you continuously remain on your path and apply tenacity and determination in every step of the process. The cosmos will lend its power intimately to encourage you throughout your journey.

Ask Yourself: What do you envision for your future and how will you begin acting and programming yourself to achieve this exalted intention in your life?

I Affirm: Today, I will visually play the motion picture of my success in my mind, leaving out no details. I will feel, see, smell, touch, and hear my success.

DECEMBER **19**   *"Anger blows out the lamp of the mind."*

— **Robert Ingersoll**

Meditation: Of course, anger is a normal human emotion; however, the key is to express the anger and work on letting it go as soon as possible. To allow anger to linger within your being is a dangerous matter. Anger hinders you from accessing your spirit and distorts your judgment profusely. Anger tears away at your ability and capacity to think clearly and feel happiness. Anger and resentment will eliminate peace and contentment from your life. Holding on to anger is a definite guarantee to an extremely low quality of life including decreased physical health, depression, frustration, rage, helplessness, and countless other negative energies that poison your soul. There is nothing productive or effective about holding on to anger and harboring resentments for any significant period of time. Each day you must cleanse yourself of the debris of anger and other toxins that threaten to take away your quality of living.

Ask Yourself: How can you express your anger effectively and move on with your life today?

I Affirm: Today, If I feel anger I will effectively deal with it and return to my natural state of peace and tranquility.

DECEMBER **20**   *"The richest person is the one who is contented with what he has."*

— **Robert C. Savage**

Meditation: You can of course spend your life accumulating more and more STUFF, however, that does not allow you the time to enjoy the things in your life that truly matter. Look around at the famous people, the so-called "great" people, the rich people, and all the additional role models of our time; if you go by the theory of accumulating things to make you happy this would mean that all these people would be content. Although, what we notice are an abundance of miserable famous, rich, and "great" people throughout the world. If you want to focus entirely on accumulating wealth in material riches, be prepared to experience a great deal of suffering.

Ask Yourself: Will you enjoy and value what truly matters today or will you keep amassing mountainous stacks of insignificant worldly possessions?

I Affirm: Today, I will make it a priority to genuinely enjoy the things in my

DECEMBER **21** *"Learn to let go. That is the key to happiness."*
— **Buddha**

Meditation: Throughout our lifetime, we collect and carry around all kinds of excess emotional baggage. This continues to cause suffering on a daily basis. Let go of the past and you will begin to have the ability to savor the present moment. Release the excessive burden of the past and experience the liberation and the freedom that is freely available to you. You are meant as a human being to live each moment with tranquility and autonomy, however, carrying the baggage of your history makes this an impossibility.

Ask Yourself: Can you let go of some of the burdensome and torturous past today and feel the exultation of being a bit lighter?

I Affirm: Today, I will embrace the ecstasy of the present moment and free myself of the baggage of the past.

DECEMBER **22** *"The next time you're off to work, dreading the day ahead, stop yourself. Decide, just for one day, to think in a whole new way."*
— **Ben Stein**

Meditation: The process of change is initiated by doing things differently for just one day. It certainly cannot be harmful to decide today to do whatever it takes to discover some pleasure in work, to be creative, and learn from those individuals around you that usually annoy you. Make a promise to yourself today to feel the peace and joy of your capacity to actually be able to work and have a job. Keep in mind others throughout the world do not have the opportunity to even go to work or receive a paycheck. Some actually do not even eat on a regular basis. Be grateful today and change the way you perceive your life.

Ask Yourself: Can you decide to have a spectacular day today no matter what happens?

I Affirm: Today, I will express gratitude for being alive and actually having the ability to read this book.

DECEMBER 23

"Life is what happens to you while your busy making other plans."

— John Lennon

Meditation: We all know those people, or may be one of them, that will surely experience happiness and contentment when they purchase a new home, a new car, get a high paying job, or go on their dream vacation. Unfortunately, when those things are accomplished happiness continues to be nonexistent. Be happy and peaceful now in this moment and stop planning happiness. Happiness is always created within, then projected to the outside world. If you cannot be joyful within, I am sorry to inform you that experiencing genuine happiness based on external means is not feasible.

Ask Yourself: Can you make a commitment to be happy right now in this very moment? What is holding you back?

I Affirm: Today, I will remember that it is I who chooses happiness; happiness is not based on an inanimate, future-based object or accomplishment.

DECEMBER 24

"Blessed are those that can give without remembering and receive without forgetting."

— Unknown Author

Meditation: During this holiday season feel the gratitude and the warming of your heart by simply giving and not expecting anything in return. The gift of giving is a sacred act that has the power to change the world. This holiday season focus on and be creative about what you will give others, give to charities, give to people you do not even know, and experience the essence of the holidays. The only requirement for a gift is to make it come from your heart and soul overflowing with your personal love and compassion. It does not have to cost much, be exquisite, or sparkle; it simply needs to be filled with human love and kindness. The best gifts I have ever received were actually rather inexpensive, but filled with thoughtfulness and affection.

Ask Yourself: Who will you give a gift to today without expecting anything in return?

I Affirm: Today, I will concentrate on giving from the bottom of my heart and soul.

DECEMBER 25

"There are three gifts you can give on a daily basis that will eventually transform all of creation; they are love, compassion and kindness."
— **Richard A. Singer, Jr.**

Meditation: Focus today on what you can contribute to humanity with these three gifts. The enormous power and possibilities that love, compassion, and kindness contain is an obvious fact, however, human beings do not step out in life and apply these principles. We sit back, observe the ruinous effects of the negative energies in the Universe, and focus on our selfish desire. Let us unite, start making a difference in humanity, and initiate the revolution of the Universe. Share your love, compassion, and kindness today and everyone around you will be content and actually feel the energy of these gifts. Start with yourself and others will follow.

Ask Yourself: How can you add your dose of love, compassion, and kindness to the world today?

I Affirm: Today, I will entirely focus my energy on dispersing love, compassion, and kindness throughout humanity.

DECEMBER 26

"Anger helps straighten out a problem like a fan helps straighten out a pile of papers."
— **Susan Marcotte**

Meditation: Anger is a terribly destructive emotion to a human being, a problem, a society, and the world as a whole if it is not expressed immediately and effectively. Some people allow anger to plague their inner core everyday for extensive periods of time. Do not get me wrong anger is a normal human emotion, but we must feel it, express it, learn from it and move on to an effective solution. Anger will create mass chaos in your life if you allow it to linger on for extended periods.

Ask Yourself: How will you effectively deal with anger in your life today?

I Affirm: Today, I will free myself from debilitating anger and ask the Universe to supply me with the strength to allow anger to flow gently through me like a soft stream running through the peaceful forest.

December

DECEMBER 27 *"Actions speak louder than words."*

— Anonymous

Meditation: If you are similar to a majority of the human race you have probably talked about many things you were going to do, were going to be, were going to achieve, but only talking and not taking the next step to get results. Today is the time to stop talking and begin walking. Just start the process and the Universe will guide you along the way. One of the most profound, but simple principles in life is keeping to your word. This will transform your thoughts, beliefs, and intentions into actions that will produce success in your life. It is very basic, but true; act upon what you wish and it will materialize in your life.

Ask Yourself: What will you begin to take action toward today in your life rather than talking about what you will do in the future? Talkers ultimately end up in coffee shops talking about what they did not get to do in their life. If you say that you would love to do something, it is your responsibility to make it happen.

I Affirm: Today, I will take action toward my dreams and desires; then there will be no reason for regrets in the future.

DECEMBER 28 *"Passion is in all great searches and is necessary to all creative endeavors."*

— W. Eugene Smith

Meditation: Passion is the key to open the door to success in your life. If you have discovered your passion, you must follow it, cultivate it, and pursue it with all the determination and persistence that you can muster up from the depths of your being. Passion is an intense fire that burns with excitement, love, joy, and begins in your heart, moves to your soul, and eventually materializes in the Universe. Passion has the power to transform your life, society, and the entire cosmos. Passion runs through all aspects of the Universe and must be connected to if humanity is to succeed.

Ask Yourself: How will you explore your burning passion today and make it a part of your design for the future?

I Affirm: Today, I will ask the Universe to guide me in pursuit of my all-consuming passion.

DECEMBER **29**

*"Let your heart guide you.
It whispers so listen closely."*
— Molly Goode

Meditation: Our hearts are passionate guides to living a life of extraordinary purpose. Our heart always communicates with honesty and vibrancy. Do not allow your dishonest and selfish ego to interfere with pursuing what your heart contains. Allow yourself to honor, embrace, and cherish all expressions of your heart, for they come directly from the universal source of love and compassion. Your heart knows who you are and is excited to guide you in your journey of the soul.

Ask Yourself: How will you trust in your heart along your journey today?

I Affirm: Today, I will rely on the language of my heart to guide me toward my destined purpose.

DECEMBER **30**

*"Not he who has much is rich,
but he who gives much."*
— Erich Fromm

Meditation: The yesteryears as well as the present moments illuminate the fact that those who are monetarily and materially wealthy can actually be extremely miserable, dissatisfied, and depressed. In fact, some have actually chosen to end their lives. Take heed to this lesson and realize that materially goods and fortune do not do too much for the human being's soul. Giving cultivates the heart and soul and satisfies an individual more than any material thing can ever achieve. Do not rely on the destructive and deadly ego for the truth about reality; It will often lead you astray along a weary and ruinous journey.

Ask Yourself: Who will you give to today rather than seeking fortunes and riches for yourself?

I Affirm: Today, I will access the limitless power of giving from deep within my spiritual being.

DECEMBER 31

"First we form habits, then they form us. Conquer your bad habits, or they'll eventually conquer you."
— **Dr. Rob Gilbert**

Meditation: Think deeply and honestly about the habits that you have created in your life and how they dictate what you do on a daily basis. Think carefully and choose one that you would like to make a commitment to change. It is important to list the pros and cons of continuing this habit, then begin thinking about change, followed by making a firm decision and allegiance to take action one day at a time.

Ask Yourself: What habit will you begin to change one day at time when the clock strikes midnight? Take the time today to painstakingly contemplate if you truly want to change. If not, wait until later, the choice is yours and the rewards of change will be worth all the effort and sacrifice, but you must have a sincere desire to change. Good luck, but most importantly, do not relinquish your determination and passion to change. Best of "luck" in the new year and your brand new life.

I Affirm: Today, I will ask the Universe for the guidance and strength to persist on my new path of personal transformation.

ABOUT THE AUTHOR

Richard A. Singer, Jr. is a practicing psychotherapist living in the Cayman Islands. He is formerly of Pennsylvania and has a Master's Degree in Clinical Psychology and is currently working on his Doctorate Degree in Psychology at Saybrook Graduate School and Research Center. His daily inspirations have been included as part of *Chicken Soup for the Recovering Soul,* from the best selling Chicken Soup series. His own recovery from addiction and depression impassioned him to help others find courage, determination and peace, and has made what some would call "work" the love and purpose of his life.

To learn more about Mr. Singer and explore updated information, visit his website

www.yourdailywalk.org. or e-mail him at RAS9999@aol.com.

In addition, please join the him for down-to-earth interactive discussions about the suggested monthly readings, daily quotes, meditations affirmations, and journaling sections of the book on his Amazon.com blog.